Cost-Benefit Analysis

Other books by D. W. Pearce

Cost—Benefit Analysis: Theory and Practice
(with A. K. Dasgupta)
Capital Investment Appraisal (with C. J. Hawkins)
The Dictionary of Modern Economics (editor)
The Economics of Natural Resource Depletion (editor)
The Social Appraisal of Projects (with C. A. Nash)

Cost–Benefit Analysis

Second Edition

D. W. Pearce
*Department of Political Economy,
University College, London*

St. Martin's Press   New York

All rights reserved. For information, write:
St. Martin's Press, Inc., 175 Fifth Avenue, New York, NY 10010
Printed in Great Britain
Published in the United Kingdom by The Macmillan Press Ltd
First published in the United States of America in 1983

ISBN 0–312–17008–4

Library of Congress Cataloging in Publication Data

Pearce, David William.
  Cost-benefit analysis.

  Includes bibliographical references.
  1. Cost effectiveness. I. Title.
HD47.4.P42 1983   658.1'554   83–14268
ISBN 0–312–17008–4

For **Corin** and **Daniel**

Contents

Contents

Preface and Acknowledgements

In 1971 I published a short text on cost—benefit analysis which, warts and all, has enjoyed some considerable commercial success. It was followed a year later by Ajit Dasgupta's and my *Cost—Benefit Analysis: Theory and Practice* (Macmillan, 1972), which remains in print. In the late 1970s it was more than obvious that the small text, which was intended largely as a student revision book, needed substantial updating and correction. That project, like Topsy, growed and the end-result was my text with Chris Nash, *The Social Appraisal of Projects: A Text in Cost—Benefit Analysis* (Macmillan, 1981). Equally obvious, however, was the fact that we had gone well beyond the publisher's instruction to write a successor to the small cost—benefit book. Since sales of the 1971 book continued to be reasonably buoyant, it was evident that there was still a market demand for a brief 'guidebook' to CBA. This 'new edition' of the 1971 text is that replacement, but it has been *completely* rewritten. What remains, however, is the central message of the 1971 text: that there is no unique way of carrying out cost—benefit studies, nor should there be, and on that I remain totally unrepentant, despite the strictures of my colleagues such as Professor Ed Mishan who have so eloquently argued the opposite but not, in my view, convincingly. Other features remain, I hope, unusual enough to attract the same audience that approved of the 1971 edition.

Preface and Acknowledgements

My debts to others are, literally, too numerous to mention. Many of my working partners will see sections that owe much to their influence. Other colleagues may note passages in which I have especially gone out of my way to explain and defend views which I know they disapproved of, and may still do so. However, while not implicated in the errors that may remain, I must record enormous gratitude to Chris Nash for many years of 'internal' debate on cost—benefit, and to my good friend Jean-Philippe Barde of the OECD, Paris, for insisting always that technique without relevance explains rather too much of the disrepute that academic economists bring on themselves. The text was written during my last year at Aberdeen University. But for Winnie Sinclair, an embodied technological revolution in herself, this and so much else would simply never have appeared. I am forever grateful.

Aberdeen and London   D. W. PEARCE
March 1983

The Foundations of Cost–Benefit Analysis

Cost–benefit analysis (CBA) excites opinion among economists and non-economists. Referring to the attempt by CBA to express all benefits and costs in monetary terms, even where we have no market in the benefit or cost in question, and, indeed, *especially* where we have no such markets, Self (1970) has remarked:

> Cost–benefit analysis gets its plausibility from the use of a common monetary standard, but the common value of the £ derives from exchange situations. Outside such situations, common values cannot be presumed, and symbol and reality become easily confused . . . To call these judgements £s is to engage in a confidence trick – to exploit the ordinary man's respect for the yardstick of money in what are actually non-monetary situations. (Self, 1970, p. 8)

The same central feature of CBA worried Schumacher (1973):

> To press non-economic values into the framework of the economic calculus, economists use the method of cost/benefit analysis. This is

generally thought to be an enlightened and progressive development, as it is at least an attempt to take account of costs and benefits which might otherwise be disregarded altogether. In fact, however, it is a procedure by which the higher is reduced to the level of the lower and the priceless is given a price. It can therefore never serve to clarify the situation and lead to an enlightened decision. All it can do is lead to self-deception or the deception of others; for to undertake to measure the immeasurable is absurd and constitutes but an elaborate method of moving from preconceived notions to forgone conclusions . . . what is worse, and destructive of civilisation, is the pretence that everything has a price or, in other words, that money is the highest of all values. (Schumacher, 1973, pp. 41–2)

It would be unfair to the critics to suggest that the sole focus of all their misgivings is the attempt to put money values on non-marketed things. There are many other stated objections, ranging from discrimination against future generations, an overly narrow definition of what any policy decision should be about, the alleged neglect of income distribution, the potential for 'rule by experts' given the complexity of any rigorously executed CBA, and so on. Many of these objections will be analysed in the course of this book. The remarks by Self and Schumacher, however, serve to indicate that some care needs to be taken in understanding just what the basis of CBA is.

We may begin with a definition. We define a *rational choice* as one in which an individual chooses an option when the gains from the action in question exceed the losses. For gains and losses we can use the terms 'advantages' and 'disadvantages', 'pros' and 'cons', or 'benefits' and 'costs'. Further, we shall leave it to the individual to define what he or she means by gains and losses. In particular, they need not be gains and losses to the individual in question. They could already embody some degree of 'altruism' – concern for others. Next, we shall produce a second definition: 'society' is nothing more than the collection of individuals who make it up. There is to be no concern with entities such as the 'state', in

2

the sense that shall not regard the 'state' or 'society' as being something *in addition to* the sum of people who comprise it.

CBA is a procedure for:

1. measuring the gains and losses to individuals, using money as the measuring rod of those gains and losses
2. aggregating the money valuations of the gains and losses of individuals and expressing them as a net social gains or losses.

Given the definitions of 'rationality' and 'society', we can therefore say that a rational *social decision* is one in which the benefits to society (i.e. the sum of the people in society) exceed the costs. Note that use of the term 'rational' seems a little emotive. Few of us would like to think we are not rational in our choices. But rationality and morality are not at all the same thing. Judging that action X will give me more benefits than costs and choosing X as a result is not the same thing as saying that X is a 'morally correct' action. By depriving, say, a major charity of money I could otherwise have given it, my choice may seem distinctly morally unacceptable to others. In the same way, the summation of a whole set of choices by many individuals may give a result which the 'state' or government thinks is not right. As a procedure for aggregating the preferences of our set of individuals, we can establish something of fundamental importance at the outset: *CBA makes no claim to produce morally correct decisions.*

What CBA produces, and what is morally correct, may coincide if, and only if, we adopt a further rule, namely that some aggregated set of preferences of individuals is the morally correct way of making decisions. In some circumstances the two may well coincide. In others, government will often reserve the right to 'overrule' group preferences. In still others, and these are surely the majority, governments will at least wish to know what the preferences of the individuals who make up society are. It is in this sense that CBA is an 'input', an 'aid', an 'ingredient' of decision-making. It does not *supplant* political judgement.

Now, there can be no doubt that there are unscrupulous economists, along with unscrupulous politicians, philosophers and engineers. If, therefore, CBA has been exaggerated in terms of its role in decision-making, it may be that there are those who have not practised its tenets properly. Equally, we must investigate to see why it should be so easy to produce the kind of result that has clearly irritated and offended the likes of Self and Schumacher. Their worries arose, in particular, because of (a) the attempt to apply the market-place philosophy to non-market situations, and (b) their doubts about the values expressed in the market-place as a guide to anything that can be described as morally correct. These are familiar objections to CBA, and the two separate strands of concern are frequently confused. If (b) is correct, for example, and we cannot ascribe 'morality' to market-place evaluations, then the valuations obtained by using the same procedures in contexts where there are no (obvious) markets must also be immoral. But objection (a) could still be made while (b) is regarded as morally acceptable. In this case, we are more likely to be arguing that things not traded in markets are, in some sense, 'special' and hence not open to valuation in money terms. Or it could be that the objection is a practical one as to whether the specific techniques used really are capturing the 'full' value in the non-market situation.

Value judgements and CBA

We have argued that CBA is a technique, as yet undefined, for aggregating the preferences of individuals. CBA makes no claim to be morally binding, for the simple reason that what is moral need not coincide with what people want. That should be sufficient to establish the role of CBA. It does not make political judgement redundant because there is no *necessary* relationship between those judgements and the wants of individuals. (We shall not investigate the issue of how political judgements relate to moral judgements!) Notice that this

4

already removes some part of the objections raised by Self and Schumacher, for it is odd to speak of deceiving the people whose valuations make up the result obtained by the CBA. If the objection is that CBA does not *in practice* reflect individuals' valuations, that is a quite different objection and one that raises a much larger area of concern about how we 'test' for the accuracy of any results. We return to that issue later.

In what way, then, does CBA seek to aggregate individual preferences? It does this by taking the market-place as the prime context in which those preferences are expressed. The medium through which they are expressed is money. It is important to realise the reason for this. It has nothing to do with being obsessed with money, and everything to do with the *fact* that markets are the only contexts in which individuals express millions of preferences daily. The political system does not begin to compare. We would have to have endless referendums and elections to get remotely near the complexity of the market-place, whether it be the local fish market, the Stock Exchange or something as complex as the foreign exchange market comprising the world's financial institutions and a very large number of telephones, telex machines and computer display units.

Within these markets countless individuals express their preferences *for* or *against* goods and services. They vote for them by buying them and against them by not buying them. The means that they use to express their votes is, of course, money. Those votes could be expressed in terms of any measuring-rod. It so happens that money has evolved as a convenient measuring-rod. Had it been cowrie shells or camel bells they would still have been 'money', which is simply a word for the medium of exchange. In this respect there can be no objection to a technique which seeks to elicit preferences expressed in terms of money. If that remains an objection, we must surely conclude that the critic has not understood at all the evolution of economies. But that cannot be what worried Self and Schumacher. We get a little closer when we consider that money is a medium of exchange *and* a store of value in terms of income and wealth. What this means is that the preferences expressed in the market-place are conditional on the possession of money. That is, those preferences will be weighted by the market power conferred on individuals through their possession of money. This is part of what Schumacher means when he refers to the 'pretence' that 'money is the highest of all values'. As we shall see, there are ways of adjusting our CBA for this kind of concern, but for the moment we should pause to see what our analysis has revealed.

First, it is evident that CBA involves the aggregation of individuals' assessments of the costs and benefits to them of a given action, policy, project or programme. This means that we have implicitly accepted that CBA results will, if properly derived, reflect individuals' preferences. If CBA is then an input to the procedure of deciding what a decision-maker ought to do, then CBA is itself 'normative' and rests on at least one value judgement or normative statement, namely that it is a good thing that individuals' preferences should count. Note that a normative judgement or statement *recommends* and implies that what is recommended is 'good'. While we can ask 'why' we should do something, it eventually becomes rather redundant to ask why something is good. Our views as to what is and what is not good will diverge.

Second, by looking at the role that money actually pays in the *measure* of preferences, we observed that market-places operate on the basis that those with more money have more say than those without. Note the contrast here with a political vote which, in an ideal world, is unrelated to income or wealth. If we are to leave the aggregated preferences in the market-place unadjusted, it follows that they will reflect the structure of market power, or, to put it another way, the distribution of income. If we are to afford CBA its role in the decision-making procedure, then, we must add a second value judgement, namely that the distribution of income used to weight the preferences of individuals is in some sense the best one. In short, the existing distribution is good. (Indeed, we have to go a little further and say it is the best.)

Now, the two normative judgements that emerge require restating. They are:

1. individual preferences should count
2. those preferences should be weighted by the existing distribution of income.

That individual preferences should count implies that social decision rules reflecting individual preferences are 'good' rules. This is appealing in that it obviously defines the basis of what we might call 'simple democracy'. Judgement (1) is thus the basic requirement of democratic sensitivity, or, as it is best known in economics, consumer sovereignty. What is morally appealing about (2)? Perhaps the existing distribution of income reflects the distribution of effort in the economy and we might invoke a principle that people deserve a 'proper' reward for their effort. Against this we might point out that the existing distribution of income already contains that reward; what we are arguing about is whether CBA should *also* reflect that distribution. After all, if CBA is used to guide decisions, this is tantamount to saying that those who have already been rewarded will be rewarded again. Obviously, the debate over (2) could go on, but one thing is clear. We do not have to accept (2) in its particular form as stated here. Equally, we cannot refuse to adopt *some* judgement such as (2). For example, if we reject (2) and say that all the preferences recorded will somehow be 'equalised' to net out the influence of market power, then we have rejected (2) in its stated form but have replaced it with a variant of (2). The only rule we seem to have for selecting one variant of (2) rather than another is its 'moral appeal'. CBA can be constructed in different ways according to whether we combine (1) with (2), or (1) with some variant of (2). But of course we could reject (1) on the grounds that individuals are poor judges of their gains and losses. This 'paternal' argument would then mean that we would have to substitute another set of preferences for (1), perhaps the preferences of some set of experts or those who have the final responsibility for decision-making. Now, if we accept this line of thought, what happens to judgement (2)? We now have to replace that with some judgement to the effect that each expert's valuation is equally important or that there is some weighting of judgements (according to seniority, peer group review?).

We conclude that CBA requires TWO normative (value) judgements. The first states that preferences count, but requires careful qualification about WHOSE PREFERENCES are to count. The second must say how the preferences are to be weighted.

We are now in a position to make some brief, but important, observations.

First, there are two, and only two, forms of judgement required. This may be contrasted with the proliferation of value judgements suggested by some authors (e.g. Peacock, 1973).

Second, if we decide to adjust *either* value judgement we have not engaged in any underhand or illicit activity. There are no rules for choosing between ultimate value judgements. Choice is determined by 'moral appeal'. Appeals to the existence of 'virtual constitutions' (Mishan, 1974) cannot be more than this.

Third, CBA is a normative procedure. Not only is this *not* a limitation, it actually reflects the nature of economics itself and, some would say, *all* science (Katouzian, 1980). A frequent charge against CBA is that it is 'subjective'. This is a confusion. As value judgement (1) indicates, it is the subjective preferences of individuals that we are seeking. In that trivial sense it is indeed 'subjective'. But if the criticism is meant to be that the analyst himself can influence the outcome in some arbitrary way, then we have to point out that there is always the scope for falsification in any analytical technique, but that scope is not part of the conceptual structure of CBA.

Fourth, and following on from the earlier points, what value judgements *are* chosen must be made clear. If they are hidden in the analysis, then the charge of 'subjectivity' in practice will have substance. We can go further. Not only should the judgements be made clear, but the outcome of the

CBA should be recalculated to show the effects of changes in the value judgements. We should practise 'value judgement sensitivity analysis' (Nash, Pearce and Stanley, 1975).

Money, preferences and 'non-markets'

So far, then, we have established, in outline form, the philosophical basis of CBA. In so doing we would argue that we have revealed some sources of misunderstanding in the quotations given at the outset. And in so far as the objection to the use of the measuring-rod of money is based on money as income or wealth, we shall see later how it is possible to adjust for that objection. But the quotations also indicate a concern about extending the measurement of preferences to so-called 'non-market situations'. We need to dwell on this issue briefly.

The preferences expressed in markets are revealed as offers of money in exchange for some benefit received. The bid made by the buyer of the benefit shows up as a willingness to pay for the benefit, conditional on his ability to pay (income or wealth). But what is *actually* paid could well be less than this willingness to pay. It cannot be more because then the individual will simply record a preference against the good or service: he will not buy it. But given that the actual price paid is determined by the interaction of many buyers and a few or many sellers, there will be individuals whose willingness to pay exceeds the price they actually pay. As we shall see, this excess of willingness to pay (WTP) over price is *consumer surplus*. Since the sum of money actually paid involves a loss for the individual, then that loss is the 'cost' of the purchase. We have a basic element of CBA in this simple example, for we can write, *for the individual*:

$$WTP = Price\ paid$$

$$Individual's\ net\ benefit = Consumer\ surplus$$

9

We shall return to this formulation when we look at the measurement of benefits.

Now apply this procedure to a situation in which there is no obvious market in the good or service. To find the net benefit to any individual of a non-marketed benefit such as peace and quiet, clean air, visual amenity, the preservation of wildlife, and so on, we need to find WTP and price, but since there is no market there is no set of actual transactions to provide us with price. The price, in fact, is zero. Indeed, this is just how we refer to these types of benefits. They are 'unpriced' or 'zero-priced'. But note that this is entirely different from saying that WTP is zero. Indeed, it needs only a moment's reflection to indicate that all the benefits we have listed have a *positive* WTP. That is, if there were a market, individuals would be willing to pay for the benefits obtained.

In fact, the reference often made to 'unmarketed' goods is slightly misleading. There are no markets in the goods or services as such, but there are often markets in other goods or services which are influenced by the valuations placed on the benefits of the unmarketed goods. These are *surrogate markets*. Two examples will suffice. First, while we have no obvious market in peace and quiet, we do have a housing market. If people buy and sell houses and are influenced by the extent to which a specific property is in a quiet location or not, then we should be able to observe the workings of the housing market and see if it 'reveals' the WTP for peace and quiet. As a second example, consider the highly emotive issue of the 'value of human life'. Resistant though many of us might be to the idea of valuing life, it is clear that individuals often do accept sums of money in return for an increase in the *risk* of death. One example might be premia added to wages for working in a dangerous occupation. Notice that it is not 'life' itself that is being valued by these premia, but the risk associated with the extra danger. Note also that this is not an example of WTP but rather 'willingness to accept' for the increased risk. Since the increased risk is the opposite of a benefit – i.e. a cost – this measure should strike us as accept-

10

able and consistent with the procedure so far developed. So, our first response to those who argue that there are 'no valuations' in certain kinds of goods and services must be to say that the absence of a direct market is not at all the same thing as the absence of an indirect market, and that the absence of a direct market does *not* mean that preferences and valuations are not made. If the logic of using market-place valuations is accepted, it is difficult to see how it can be rejected for surrogate markets.

This leaves us with goods and services whose values are not revealed in any market, obvious or surrogate. The value of a blue whale would seem to be a case in point. There is a commercial market in whales, but we would rightly reject the market price of the whale as oil and blubber as reflecting the aggregate of individuals' WTPs for the blue whale, for we know that there are many hundreds of thousands, perhaps millions, of people who value the whale in its natural state, even though they may only have seen one on their televisions, or in photographs. In such contexts we have two options. We can leave the issue 'unvalued' and say that we have no conceptual technique for working out the WTP for blue whales, or we can *invent* a market. To do this we can hypothesise a situation in which individuals vote for preservation of the blue whale and ask them what they *would* be willing to pay *if* there was a market in whales which was as open to them as it was to whalers. We can all envisage the practical difficulties, but for the moment we are concerned to know if the absence of an actual market reflecting all our valuations imposes any conceptual problem on our logic of finding WTP. It would seem not, and there are indeed a fair number of experiments in establishing such *hypothetical* or *'experimental' markets.*

How, then, does all this relate to the view that goods and services which do not have direct markets are somehow 'different' from other goods and services? For these goods to be so special that we cannot apply even the conceptual logic of CBA to them requires us to establish that any of the above means of calculating WTP would seriously mistate the true benefits. But that presents us with a pervasive methodological problem. For we shall not be able to tell whether we have the 'right' valuation unless we have some *other* measuring-rod against which to compare our measure of WTP. But if we had some other measuring-rod, we would surely not need the WTP approach in the first place. While we shall see that it is possible to compare the results obtained from surrogate market analyses with experimental (hypothetical) markets in certain cases, in most of them we shall have to rely on some form of judgement as to the extent to which any technique used captures all the preferences that should be included. Thus part of what Schumacher had in mind in his own remark quoted earlier is that economic techniques such as CBA will fail to identify certain values. Universally, CBA speaks of values as attributes of things as perceived by humankind. We make no attempt to include the preferences of blue whales in our analyses. CBA is 'anthropocentic'. If that is the source of criticism, then it should be acknowledged, and the point made earlier, that CBA cannot be presented as something which is synonymous with moral correctness, must be invoked. If the criticism is that we have neglected some value of the good or service *to* humankind, then it is a charge of omission and that is important within the rules that CBA has established for itself. What Schumacher was worrying about was CBA's neglect of the environment as a *system* for supporting human life, and since the environment is invariably the good which has, at best, surrogate markets and, more usually, no markets, there is a good reason to agree with Schumacher that there is a deficiency in the way CBA operates.

As a final comment in this chapter, we may observe from the way the discussion has progressed that a 'benefit' is *any* gain to any individual included in the group in question. That gain may accrue in some money form, or it may accrue as some sense of pleasure or happiness. In the language of economics, we require only that it be some *welfare* or *utility* gain. Similarly, a 'cost' is not defined in terms of a money flow. It is, in fact, anything that imparts a loss of utility or welfare.

Notice that this will subsume, say, the money value of the resources used to build a motorway or whatever, because those resources could have been used to give welfare gains elsewhere or from some other project. In this sense a cost is always a forgone benefit. Indeed, it should now be evident that cost in the context of CBA always means *opportunity cost*. One problem which is not readily resolvable in conceptual terms is quite *who* counts when calculating costs and benefits. One is tempted to say that a nation's boundary sets the limits on who should count if we are building a road or an airport and using up the nation's resources. But that may not be sound reasoning if the roads and airport are used by persons from other nations. The use of national boundaries appears even less defensible if we are looking at the costs and benefits of a policy to control sulphur dioxide emissions into the atmosphere and we discover that the cheapest way (in terms of resources) is to build high chimneys and allow the sulphur dioxide to travel across to other countries. What may yield net benefits to the 'emitting' nation may do so only because that nation has 'exported' the pollution to another country. And if we reconsider our example of the blue whale, it would seem necessary to set no national boundaries at all regardless of where the blue whale is most often seen. There are in fact no clear rules on setting the 'boundaries' for a CBA. Most often it will be obvious, but on other occasions it will not be.

2

The Origins of Cost–Benefit Analysis

While the underlying *theory* of CBA can be traced back to some welfare economics of the nineteenth century, the *practice* of CBA can be said to date from the introduction of the Flood Control Act 1936 in the USA. It seems fair to say that that Act owed little or nothing to the body of welfare economics theory that had emerged by the time of the Act's introduction; indeed, as we shall see, the placing of CBA in a firm conceptual framework occurred after the Act and particularly in light of certain theoretical developments at the end of the 1930s. The Flood Control Act determined that the control of flood waters was 'in the interests of the general welfare'. And it went on to state a most general rule to the effect that the Federal Government 'should improve or participate in the improvement of navigable waters . . . for flood control purposes *if the benefits to whomsoever they accrue are in excess of the estimated costs*' (our italics). Too much must not be read into the Flood Control Act. First, the reference to the unrestricted nature of the benefits that

14

should be taken into account was not matched by a similar coverage for costs. It is clear that the Act was referring to the costs of construction and did not embrace the wider idea of a cost as *any* loss of welfare. Second, the Act itself makes no further mention of the 'benefits *minus* costs' principle and commentators seem generally agreed that many of the projects subsequently sanctioned after the Act would not have passed the benefit—cost rule as it was developed. Third, the meaning of the term 'benefits' was also not made clear.

The next landmark was the so-called 'Green Book' of 1950 produced by the US Federal Inter-Agency River Basin Committee and which attempted to instill some agreed set of rules for comparing costs and benefits. A further attempt at formalisation came with the US Bureau of Budget's *Budget Circular A—47* in 1952. These were early attempts, and they were followed by the general introduction of economic techniques into budget management in the USA across many areas of expenditure. This process was aided by the emerging literature from the Rand Corporation, which had devoted considerable time to the development of rules of resource allocation in military spending. Here the benefits were expressed in terms of 'national security' or, in more macabre terms, destructive capability. But the important development was in the use of procedures for minimising the money cost of a given level of activity — the beginnings of 'cost-effectiveness analysis' (CEA), by which the benefit is measured in some physical units, or is simply stated as a policy objective, and the costs are expressed in monetary units. At the very least, then, alternative means of achieving the same end could be ranked in terms of the ratio of cost to effectivensss (C/E), and the same ratio could be used for projects with differing benefits as a guide to judgement. Thus both CBA and CEA began their practical lives as aids to government decision-making.

We observed that the Flood Control Act actually preceded the developments in welfare economics that eventually came to give CBA its economic foundations. During the 1950s in the USA there was a gradual and somewhat unintegrated convergence of theory and practice. The year 1958 marked the publication of three highly important works, by Eckstein (1958), Krutilla and Eckstein (1958), and McKean (1958), all ostensibly to do with water resource development in the USA but each containing important links to the theoretical literature of welfare economics. The basic linkages were (a) the construal of a benefit as any *gain* in welfare (utility) and a cost as any *loss* in welfare, (b) the concept of cost as *opportunity cost*, so that, strictly, the benefit—cost rule became one of (ideally) maximising the difference between measured benefits and the forgone benefits from the project 'displaced' by the chosen project, and (c) the rooting of the idea of maximising net benefits in the Pareto improvement rule. The Pareto rule stated a virtual tautology to the effect that 'society' was better off if at least some of its members were made better off and no one was made worse off. Note that the concept of society as the sum of the individuals in it is explicit in this rule. But since no project is likely ever to meet this rule, reference was made to the modification of it introduced by Kaldor (1939) and Hicks (1939). The so-called Kaldor—Hicks rule stated that any project should be sanctioned if it improved the welfare of some people, even though others might lose, provided those who gained could compensate those who lost and still have some benefit left over. Expressed in this way, the rule, or 'compensation test', is simple. Imagine that we can put money values on the benefits and costs, and that benefits accrue to five people and sum to 100 units. Costs accrue to twenty people and sum to 90 units. Then, in theory, the five beneficiaries can transfer 90 units to the losers, and they will still have 10 units of net benefit. The losers will be fully compensated for their initial loss so that they are no worse off. The compensation principle thus establishes a potentially attractive way of making the Pareto rule operational. Notice that it is not affected by the numbers of people in the gaining or losing groups, nor is anything said about *who* the groups are (rich, poor, etc.).

Reference was made in this new literature to one of the

salient criticisms of the Kaldor—Hicks rule, given by Scitovsky (1941), to the effect that a project sanctioned by the rule could give rise to a subsequent situation in which those who had lost could now 'compensate' those who had gained to move back to the pre-project state. That this could happen arises from the fact that the project may change the distribution of income and hence the pattern of relative prices. At the *initial* set of prices the project is judged worth while, but at the *new* set of prices emerging after the project is undertaken we can hypothesise a project involving a move back to the initial position and this project may be sanctioned by the very same test used to justify the move away from that initial position. A more formal statement of the compensation test and Scitovsky's criticism is given in the appendix to this chapter. While Scitovsky's criticism was acknowledged, it was largely ignored in what now seemed to be a relentless advance by CBA and CEA into the appraisal of government expenditures. The context of the techniques – government spending – was natural because government, as opposed to the private sector, is supposedly concerned with the wider general welfare of the population. There is in fact nothing in CBA which forbids its application to private-sector investments. Indeed, such procedures are useful indicators of the extent to which private and socially efficient decisions diverge. But, by and large, CBA remained, and has remained, in the domain of the public sector.

The other major American work to emerge in the early 1960s was that produced by the Harvard Water Resource Program (Maass, 1962), which forged closer linkages with the underlying welfare theory. Thereafter, countless articles and books appeared, and CBA also arrived in the United Kingdom with the application of the technique to the London—Birmingham motorway, the M1 (Beesley *et al.*, 1960). In 1967 a UK Government White Paper gave formal recognition to the existence of cost—benefit analysis and assigned it a limited role for nationalised industries (UK Government, 1967). The essence of the directive was that nationalised industries should

17

operate on a commercial basis, and should seek an 8 per cent rate of return on new investment. Returns were, however, to be measured in terms of financial revenues with the exception of situations in which 'there are grounds for thinking that the social costs or benefits do diverge markedly from those associated with the alternatives' (i.e. alternative investments). In these cases the government would carry out some type of cost—benefit analysis.

In the late 1960s CBA was extended to less developed countries with the publication of a *Manual of Industrial Project Analysis* (Little and Mirrlees, 1969). The *Manual* was prepared for the Organisation for Economic Co-operation and Development (OECD) and was updated and revised in 1974 (Little and Mirrlees, 1974), while in 1972 the United Nations Industrial Development Organisation (UNIDO) published its own guidelines (Marglin *et al.*, 1972), different in detail but essentially the same in philosophy. In 1975 came the World Bank's guidelines, which were heavily reliant on the earlier work of Little and Mirrlees (Squire and van der Tak, 1975). CBA also gained additional impetus with the environmental revolution. Since costs and benefits were defined to include all welfare gains and losses, the complex task of applying CBA in contexts where measurement problems were severe attracted many researchers. Unquestionably, for the comparatively small sums spent on this dimension of CBA research, the returns were very high. But, arguably, CBA did little to influence environmental policy as such. As an example the US Clean Air Act 1970 and the Amendments to it in 1977 made no mention of costs and benefits. But the main advance was in establishing a way of thinking about environmental problems from a rigorous standpoint.

Ironically, it was the advocates of the environmental movement that contributed to the poor image of CBA in the 1970s. The idea that the environment was to be subject to procedures for monetary evaluation was, and is, anathema to many who regard the preservation of environments as some kind of categorical imperative, not subject to the rules of allocative efficiency. Wilderness areas, for example, were held to 'beyond price', a phrase which alternatively seemed to mean that they possessed infinite values (an absurdity in a world of finite resources), or that, somehow, they belonged to a category of things which could not be traded with other things that are legitimately valued in terms of the measuring-rod of money. In the United Kingdom, outrage was most marked over the advice given by a statutory commission (the Roskill Commission) on the proposed location of London's Third Airport (Commission on the Third London Airport, 1971). Apart from the fact that the recommendation, based on a very detailed cost—benefit analysis, was for an inland site in a context where, politically, a coastal site was preferred, the motivating force for the condemnation of CBA lay in the marked difference between the measured costs of noise nuisance and the costs of time lost by air passengers in the air and on the ground. The former were, at the most, generous estimate, only some 0.7 per cent of the latter at the recommended site. In essence this arose from the fact that the value attributed to savings in travel time were (i) high and (ii) applied to *any* time savings whether it was thirty minutes or one minute. It is arguable that individuals only value time in 'discrete' units of, say, more than five or ten minutes, making the CBA procedure used in the study illicit. It is not the case that studies since Roskill suggest any significantly higher valuations for noise nuisance. More detail of the Roskill valuation of time and noise procedures is given in Dasgupta and Pearce (1972). Using the low comparative value of the environment in relation to saving travelling time, the critics had a field day, with CBA being described as 'nonsense on stilts' by one commentator, echoing Bentham on natural rights (Self, 1970; 1975).

In the United Kingdom, then, CBA fell into some disrepute in the 1970s, though it continued to flourish in the USA and elsewhere. Much of the criticism was misplaced, being based on simple misunderstandings of the role played by 'money' in the technique. Money as a measuring-rod for benefits and costs became confused with money as some kind of immoral or irreligious goal. At the same time, CBA had stolen a march on other disciplines equally concerned to establish their own applicability to the evaluation of road and airport expenditures, environmental policy, and so on. Once the groundwork for the attack on CBA was laid, the way was open for the advocacy of allegedly superior techniques such as *environmental impact assessment*. Writing in 1983, it seems fair to say that the wheel has come full circle. CBA has matured, and if much of the criticism of it was misplaced it is also the case that many advocates of CBA 'oversold' its attractions. Above all, the *role* of CBA is clearer in that, as Chapter 1 showed, CBA cannot be a unique rule for *making* decisions, for it is always open to us to ask whether the particular value judgements used to construct CBA are value judgements of which we approve.

One question remains in respect of this historical excursion into CBA's development. We have seen that CBA actually achieved its rationale *ex post*. The practice, as it were, preceded the theory. The harnessing of welfare theory thus added a powerful conceptual base for CBA. And yet CBA both advanced in terms of practice, and in terms of the merging of theory and practice, at a time when welfare economics itself had come under the most severe criticism. As we have seen, Scitovsky (1941) found an inherent flaw in the compensation test advanced by Kaldor and Hicks. Little (1950; 2nd edn 1957) attempted a resurrection of welfare theory through the explicit treatment of income distribution. A policy could only be judged a 'good' policy if it met the compensation test, was not subject to the Scitovsky 'reversal' procedure, and 'improved' income distribution. De Graaf (1957) produced a slim volume criticising welfare economics in such a way that many economists were satisfied that the subject was quite dead in intellectual terms. At the same time, the spirit of 'positivism' was afoot (some thirty years after it had first received its clearest statements in philosophy with A. J. Ayer's *Language, Truth and Logic*, 1936), and a good many economists denounced welfare economics, regardless of the theoretical criticisms, because of its basis in value judgements. That even the concept of allocative efficiency so basic to the meaning of economics is itself value-loaded escaped the positivists (Katouzian, 1980).

How, then, did CBA with its total reliance on welfare economics survive and flourish? Krutilla (1981) has suggested one not wholly convincing answer. It was, he says, because CBA evaluated *projects* and not *policies*. In the case of the former the distributional consequences were insignificant and hence problems such as those raised by Scitovsky did not arise. Had CBA attempted to evaluate whole policies, the distributional consequences would have been significant and CBA would have been open to an obvious intellectual attack. There is some truth in this view, but it cannot be the whole story because, in fact, there were few attempts to assess whether the distributional consequences of projects were important or not. Moreover, the kind of attack advanced by de Graaf had not only included the distributional aspect but also other criticisms, such as the use of shadow prices based on marginal cost being erroneous because of second-best problems. These could not be avoided simply by concentrating on projects.

To explain the success of CBA thus requires more than Krutilla's suggestion. Arguably, the explanation is very simple. Those who practised CBA had a real-world task to attend to. Someone had to decide on the priorities within any sub-budget of government expenditure. The niceties of academic interchange in the learned journals did little to aid those who had these tasks. Instead, it seemed that not only did CBA offer a technique for aiding the evaluative process, albeit subject to many caveats, it actually offered the *only* reasoned technique. Founded, as it is, in a very simple concept of rationality (see Chapter 1), CBA also had a fundamental attraction of reducing a complex problem to something less complex and more manageable.

Appendix: compensation tests and CBA

Figure 2.1 shows a production possibility frontier for an economy. We select a point P_1 on that frontier and observe that we now have Y_1 of good Y and X_1 of good X. This particular combination of output levels (X_1, Y_1) can be distributed in various ways between the two individuals, A and B, who comprise society. To see this, construct the Edgeworth box $OY_1P_1X_1$ for P_1 and inside it will be a contract curve which is the locus of all points of tangency of A's and B's indifference curves (e.g. I_A and I_B). If we now take the contract curve and show it in Figure 2.2 against the utility levels of A and B (U_A and U_B), it will appear as UPC_1 — a 'utility possibility curve'. But UPC_1 is only *one* utility possibility curve relating to the production possibility curve in Figure 2.1.

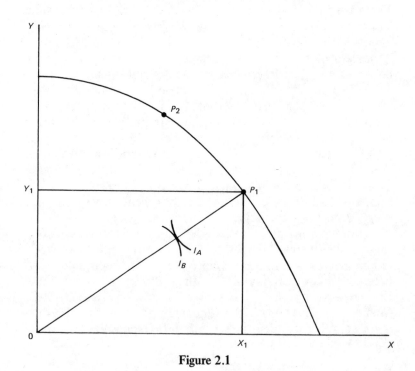

Figure 2.1

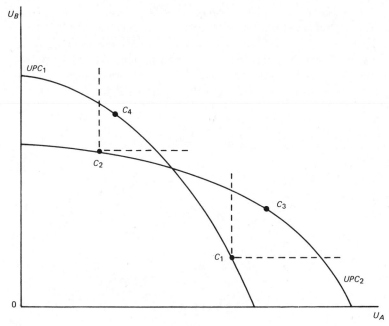

Figure 2.2

For example, if we select P_2 we shall have a new Edgeworth box and a new contract curve and hence a new utility possibility curve. Let this be UPC_2 as shown in Figure 2.2.

Now consider point C_1 in Figure 2.2 and consider a project that moves 'society' from C_1 to C_2. We appear not to be able to compare C_2 with C_1 since C_2 has improved B's utility but worsened A's. The strict Pareto rule does not apply. But at C_2 we can redistribute income and move down UPC_2 to point C_3, which is superior to C_1 because *both A and B* are better off. Effectively, then, we have changed the move from C_1 to C_2 into a hypothetical move C_1 to C_3. The move from C_2 to C_3 involves B (the gainer) compensating A (the loser), but at C_3, B is still better off than he was at C_1. Hence C_1 to C_2 is an improvement on the compensation test and we only need to observe that B *could* compensate A. He does not *actually* have to make the transfer.

23

Now, consider C_2, the situation *after* the project is implemented. We now hypothesise the 'reverse' project — i.e. moving from C_2 *back* to C_1. If the move is made, we see that at C_1 we can move up UPC_1 to C_4, which is Pareto superior to C_2. We have an oddity. The move from C_1 to C_2 is an improvement, but once at C_2 the move *back* to C_1 is also an improvement. This is the Scitovsky 'reversal paradox'.

3

The Measurement of Costs and Benefits

Chapters 1 and 2 indicated that the basic CBA rule is that an expenditure is to be judged potentially worth while if its benefits exceed its costs, where benefits and costs are defined to include any welfare gain and loss which occurs because of the expenditure on the project. But 'cost' has also to be thought of as *opportunity cost*, the benefits forgone because of the project in question. In turn, benefits are measured by the (aggregate) *willingness to pay* (WTP) of the beneficiaries. Expressed in this way, and ignoring the aggregation across many individuals, we can write:

$$\text{Net benefits} = WTP_i - WTP_j \tag{3.1}$$

where i is the project in question and j is the project 'forgone'. We wish to know how we can go from this general statement to a more detailed CBA rule.

Benefits and consumer surplus

Consider, first, the expression WTP_i. Let us suppose that project i consists of an increase in the output of product i

25

(e.g. an extra road, more railways, an additional runway at an airport, less pollution, and so on). The demand curve for *i* is shown in Figure 3.1.

Let the initial situation be that Q_1 of *i* is bought at price P_1. The project in question changes the output and price to Q_2 and P_2 respectively. Chapter 2 indicated that the WTP for Q_1 is made up of the amount *actually* paid (OQ_1XP_1) *plus* the excess of willingness to pay over actual price (P_1XZ). Clearly, then, the new total WTP for Q_2 is OQ_2YP_2 *plus* P_2YZ. The WTP for the *change* in Q (= $Q_2 - Q_1$) is thus Q_1Q_2YX. We require an expression for this area.

We can see that Q_1Q_2YX is made up of an extra amount actually paid, Q_1Q_2YW, and the triangle WYX. (Note that this triangle is the consumer surplus on the amount Q_1Q_2. It is *not* the change in consumer surplus by moving from Q_1

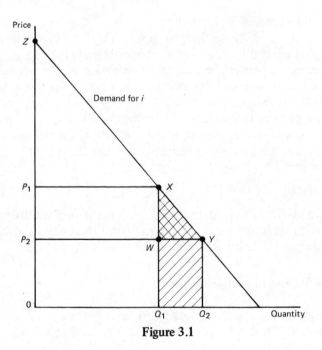

Figure 3.1

to Q_2 because this is equal to WYX *plus* the extra surplus now enjoyed on the amount OQ_1.) We can therefore calculate the change in WTP for i as

$$\Delta WTP_i = Q_1 Q_2 YW + WYX$$
$$= \Delta QP_2 + \tfrac{1}{2}Q(P_1 - P_2) \qquad (3.2)$$

The notation 'Δ' simply means 'change in', so in this case $\Delta Q = Q_2 - Q_1$. The second expression on the right-hand side assumes that the demand curve is a straight line (is 'linear') and is the formula for the area of a triangle (half base *times* altitude). We can rearrange (3.2) as

$$\Delta WTP_i = \Delta Q \left[P_2 + \frac{(P_1 - P_2)}{2} \right]$$
$$= \tfrac{1}{2}\Delta Q(P_1 + P_2) \qquad (3.3)$$

We now have our formulation for measuring the *benefit* side of equation (3.1). Benefits are equal to the change in quantity multiplied by an average of the 'before' (P_1) and 'after' prices (P_2). Now, if the change in price is very small we shall have, at the limit, $P_1 = P_2$, so that (3.3) would become

$$d\,WTP_i = PdQ \qquad (3.4)$$

where the 'd' now replaces the 'Δ' because we are thinking of very small changes in Q indeed. In fact, (3.4) defines the meaning of 'marginal willingness to pay'. *It follows that the demand curve in Figure 3.1 is a marginal willingness to pay curve*; the first person to observe this important conceptual linkage, and to coin the phrase 'consumer surplus', was Dupuit (1844).

Problems with consumer surplus

The CBA procedure requires that the willingness to pay expression in equation (3.3) be aggregated across all the individuals in question. Additionally, if there is more than one benefit, we shall have to carry out a similar exercise for the other gains obtained. We shall take it that, in order to avoid generating more complicated notation, that both of these aggregation procedures are undertaken.

But there are problems with the comparatively simple procedure just described. First, the demand curve may not be linear. If so, we shall have derived an *approximation* to WTP, not the actual amount. Obviously, this is a problem in empirical technique. If we know the demand curve, then no great problems are involved.

Second, the demand curve we have drawn in Figure 3.1 is 'Marshallian' — it simply shows quantity demanded against price. As the price of *i* falls, the real income of the consumer rises (he is better off). The problem now is that we are measuring an area under a demand curve and calling it a gain in utility when one of the factors affecting the way we *measure* utility, namely income, is itself changing. We are measuring utility with a money indicator which itself changes as the price of *i* falls. What we need is a demand curve in which this problem is removed, i.e. one in which we can see how utility varies with price, but in which money income is varied so as to keep the consumer on the same indifference curve. Our money measure will then be a unique measure of utility. We do not pursue this point here save to say that what we require is not the Marshallian curve in Figure 3.1 but a *'compensated' demand curve* of the kind introduced by Hicks (1943) and the area under which is termed a 'compensating variation'. (For a fuller explanation see Pearce and Nash, 1981, pp. 90–1.) How far this adjustment matters — i.e. to what extent significant errors in our measure of benefit are introduced by using the Marshallian demand curve to approximate consumer surplus — is an open question (but for an impressively argued case that the errors are not of great significance see Willig, 1976).

There is a third problem arising from the fact that we must aggregate surpluses to obtain an overall measure of benefit. This arises from the fact that, as the price of the good in question falls, it may well alter the demand curves for *other* products which are either substitutes or complements for it. If so, we need to know whether calculating the change in surplus for the one good is enough as a measure of the benefits of the project that give rise to that change in price. If surpluses change on other products, we should presumably take account of them. This is the problem of *estimating consumer surplus when other prices change*. The appendix to this chapter indicates the nature of the problem. It may be omitted by readers concerned only to note that the problem exists and must be accounted for in any actual CBA study. An excellent treatment of the problem is given in Just *et al.* (1982). (Indeed, for anyone concerned to pursue the welfare economics foundations of CBA, this text is highly recommended.)

Clearly, there are problems in actually estimating the consumer surplus relevant to any project. If Willig (1976) is correct, however, we shall not be dealing with large margins of error if we adopt the simple measure of surplus as the area under a Marshallian demand curve. Partly because of empirical difficulties, and partly because of the view that the errors are not large, we usually find CBA studies using 'simple' measures of surplus. In terms of theoretical rigour, however, there is a reasonable consensus that the measure we should be using is the area under a 'compensated' demand curve, i.e. one in which the income effect is removed. In turn, there are two types of compensated demand curve with the result that we can choose from *three* measures of consumer surplus: (a) the area under the Marshallian curve, or 'simple' consumer surplus; (b) the area under a demand curve that is adjusted so as to keep the consumer on his original indifference curve, known as the 'compensating variation', or CV for short; and (c) the area under a demand curve that is adjusted to keep the consumer on his subsequent indifference curve (i.e. the one after any project has been introduced), known as the 'equivalent variation', or EV for short. For the case we have analysed, where the project causes the price of the product to fall, it can be shown that CV will (generally) be less than the simple measure, which is in turn less then EV. These different measures of surplus are due to Hicks (1943). Debate still occurs on which to use. We again repeat the view that the error involved in using the simple measure is not likely to be great (Willig, 1976; Just *et al.*, 1982). For the record, CV is the measure most widely recommended in the theoretical literature (Mishan, 1975).

Costs and forgone benefits

In terms of the simple net benefit measure introduced in equation (3.1), we now have an approach to its measurement via the concept of consumer surplus (CV), albeit with some cautionary notes about how to proceed. Equation (3.1) suggests that we now need to subtract from WTP_i the amount WTP_j which is a measure of the surplus forgone on the sacrificed project (j). In fact, CBA does not proceed in this way. What it does is to substitute for WTP_j the *costs* of implementing project i. Imagine now that the only costs relevant to our project are what we have called the resource costs, the various inputs – labour, capital, etc. – used up in project i. This enables us to ignore other costs such as those imposed on third parties in the form of, say, pollution (the 'externalities'). We can easily reintroduce them. In this context, then, we now need to know whether the use of the cost of project i introduces a significant error into equation (3.1), i.e. we need to know the relationship between the cost C_i of i, C_i, and WTP_j. If they are not equal we shall have introduced an error into the basic equation (3.1).

To answer this question we can look at the inputs used in producing i. Imagine there is only *one* input, labour. (Our result will hold equally well for more than one input.) Then the *forgone output* in project j is equal to what the labour used in i *could have produced* in project j. This will be the marginal product of labour (MP_L) multiplied by the amount of labour used in j (ΔL), i.e.

$$\text{Forgone output in } j = MP_L \, \Delta L \tag{3.5}$$

and the value of this forgone output is WTP_j, or

$$WTP_j = P_j MP_L \, \Delta L \tag{3.6}$$

Now, the relationship between expression (3.6), which is WTP_j, and C_i, the cost of project i, is readily seen, since *if*

$$W_L = P_j MP_L \tag{3.7}$$

where W_L is the wage of labour, we can write:

$$WTP_j = W_L \, \Delta L = C_i \tag{3.8}$$

The equivalence between C_i and WTP_j is assured *if, and only if*, labour is paid the value of its marginal product. Generalising, the equivalence will hold if, and only if, all inputs to i are priced at their respective values of their marginal products. This will *only* be true under perfect competition. Under imperfect competition, we know that

$$P_j > \frac{W_L}{MP_L} = MC_j \tag{3.9}$$

where MC_j is the marginal cost of producing j. Hence, from (3.9), the wage will be less than the value of the marginal product (indeed, it will equal the *marginal revenue product* if the context is one of profit maximisation).

Shadow pricing

The preceding analysis suggests that we know that the equivalence of C_i and WTP_j does not hold. There will therefore be an error involved in using C_i. None the less, we shall continue to use C_i for two reasons. First, for any individual project we cannot engage in the laborious and virtually unlimited activity of estimating WTP_j, whereas we can obtain an estimate of C_i. Second, if we take the view that the error involved is serious, we can try to calculate the value of the marginal product of the inputs. The approaches to this are various and often complex. For our purposes the idea of looking for the 'proper' measure of the opportunity cost of project *i* in terms of what the various inputs would produce in a world which obeyed the efficient pricing principles derived from welfare economics is the important one: for this is known as *shadow pricing*. In the example above, shadow pricing of inputs would consist of trying to find the true opportunity cost of using the inputs in project *i*. Moreover, shadow pricing is generalisable across all inputs and outputs. Indeed, the idea that we should estimate the willingness to pay for the output of project *i* is itself nothing more than shadow pricing. It is in this context that we can derive a most important feature of CBA. This is that the prices we use in order to draw up the CBA need not bear resemblance to the prices that rule in the market for the various outputs and inputs. This is so even when there *are* markets, and the rationale for this statement is simply that the ruling prices may not reflect (marginal) opportunity cost or (marginal) willingness to pay.

When there are no obvious markets at all, the procedure of shadow pricing is one that we still pursue. If there is no obvious market in the product in question – e.g. clean air – then we can attempt to observe how individuals implicitly value clean air by looking at surrogate markets, such as the housing market. We shall be concerned to establish that any procedure for eliciting values from the observation of such markets obeys the requirements that they reflect willingness to pay. In the situation in which we have no surrogate market either, or in which we wish to test the results obtained from surrogate market studies, we can resort to experimental methods such as questionnaires. Once again, the requirement will be that the values elicited approximate willingness to pay.

It is as well to note that some cost—benefit analysts tend to use the term 'shadow price', in a more general fashion than others. Strictly, 'shadow price' relates to the valuation placed on an input or output in a context of an optimum. That optimum will tend to be constrained by limitations on the availability of some or all inputs, where the overall constraint would appear as a limitation on the sum of money available for investment in projects (a 'budget constraint'). One powerful mathematical procedure for analysing problems of optimisation in the context of constraints is known as *programming*. It is from mathematical programming that the term 'shadow price' comes. As a general statement, we can say that a shadow price measures the gain in the value of some objective if we increase expenditure on a given project by one unit. The objective in CBA is our measure of net social benefits. Hence the shadow price of any output or input is the value of the increase in net social benefit resulting from a one-unit change in that output or input. The connection with willingness to pay and opportunity cost should now be evident. The gain in net social benefit from a one-unit change in output is precisely what we have been calling 'marginal willingness to pay'. The loss from increasing inputs into our project will be the value of the output forgone in the sacrificed projects. (In programming, shadow prices emerge as the solutions to what is known as the 'dual' programme.)

We now have the basis for our cost–benefit rule. Instead of equation (3.1) we shall henceforth use the expression:

$$\text{Net benefits} = WTP_i - C_i \qquad (3.10)$$

where it will be noted that we have now substituted C_i for WTP_j.

We close this chapter with three observations:

First, we must reintroduce other costs besides the resource costs of the project. We can do this by simply remembering that C_i will be an aggregate of all the costs of project i, including the costs borne by people adversely affected by the project. To find these costs we will need to go through a further exercise of estimating the CV (compensating variation) relevant to the costs in question. Thus, if the project creates

33

pollution, we shall seek the sufferers' willingness to pay to restore their initial level of welfare before the project, or what they are willing to accept by way of compensation to tolerate the pollution.

Second, we need to remember that equation (3.10) contains a set of prices for the outputs and inputs and, regardless of whether those prices are for outputs and inputs that have associated markets, the (strictly) relevant prices are the *shadow prices*.

Third, our formula is so far 'timeless'. The next chapter introduces time into the analysis.

Appendix: consumer surplus when other prices change

We wish to know how to aggregate consumer surplus in the (likely) context where the project we are analysing causes a change in the demand curves for products which are substitutes or complements for the product in question. In what follows product X is the one subject to the initial analysis; its supply is increased because of some investment project. In terms of the simple analytics of CBA we would normally concentrate on X alone and ignore any substitute or complement for X. To see how this affects the analysis, we postulate a substitute product, Y.

The initial demand curves are shown as D_X^0 and D_Y^0 in Figure 3.2. Let the supply curve of X shift from S_X^0 to S_X^1 so that the price of X falls from P_X^0 to P_X^1. Since Y is a substitute for X, the demand curve for Y shifts leftwards from D_Y^0, thus lowering the price of Y. In turn, this will shift the demand curve for X to the left, and so on. Let the final equilibrium demand curves be D_X^1 and D_Y^2 so that the final equilibrium prices are P_X^2 and P_Y^2. What is the aggregate surplus gain from the initial price fall in X?

First, we may observe that surplus is *not* measured by the areas under the demand curves D_X^0 and D_Y^0 taken together. This is what would *appear* to be correct if we simply *added* surpluses. In fact the measure

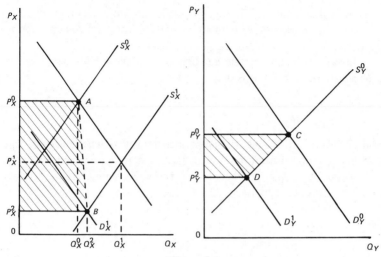

Figure 3.2

of surplus gain is ambivalent. There are three possibilities. These are:

1. the area under D_X^0 (for X) and under D_Y^2 (for Y)
2. the area under D_X^1 (for X) and under D_Y^0 (for Y)
3. assuming that prices move to their new equilibrium at the same proportionate rate, by the area

$$(P_X^0 A B P_X^2) + (P_Y^1 C D P_Y^2)$$

shown as the shaded areas in Figure 3.2.

Taking measure 3, this is equal to

$$(P_X^0 - P_X^2)Q_X^0 + \tfrac{1}{2}(P_X^0 - P_X^2)(Q_X^2 - Q_X^0) + (P_Y^0 - P_Y^1)Q_Y^1$$
$$+ \tfrac{1}{2}(P_Y^0 - P_Y^1)(Q_Y^0 - Q_Y^1)$$

or

$$\Sigma Q \Delta P + \tfrac{1}{2} \Sigma \, \Delta P \Delta Q$$

The fact that there are three (indeed, many) possibilities of measurement arises because we can choose different *paths* whereby initial prices change towards final equilibrium prices. The measure of surplus depends on the choice of path – i.e. there is what is known as *path dependence*. In measure 3, for example, the path is linear.

In fact, as long as certain conditions hold, the various measures will be equal. The prime one is that

$$\frac{\partial Q_X}{\partial P_Y} = \frac{\partial Q_Y}{\partial P_X}$$

at all sets of prices – i.e. the cross-price derivatives must be equal. This 'symmetry of substitution' will in fact hold if the demand curves in question are exclusive of income effects (i.e. are 'compensated' demand curves) but not otherwise.

4

Time, Discounting and Decision Rules

Chapter 3 concluded with a 'timeless' CBA formula which indicated that any project in which the benefits exceed the costs is a potentially 'good' project. The qualifications are (a) that the benefits and costs must be valued at shadow prices unless we have reason to believe that the error involved in not using shadow prices is small; (b) *all* costs and benefits, to whomsoever they accrue, must be accounted for; (c) the rule as formulated is indifferent between *who* receives the benefits and *who* suffers the costs (a matter we take up in Chapter 5); and (d) the excess of benefits over costs does not mean that the project should be undertaken. With respect to point (d) we shall see later that the introduction of a budget entails that we must have some *ranking* procedure.

The rationale for discounting

The costs and benefits in question will occur over time. If, for example, the benefits accrue at a constant rate over thirty

years, and the costs occur in the first five years, but not thereafter, we *could* formulate the rule that the project is worth
while if $B_1 + B_2 + \ldots + B_{30}$ is greater than $C_1 + C_2 + \ldots + C_5$. However, it is unsafe to assume that a benefit in year 2 is
regarded by society in the same way as a benefit in year 1.
Suppose the benefit is £1 in each of these years. If we are to
treat them identically, it will be quite legitimate to add up
the benefits (and costs) in the way we have just done. But
we have two basic interrelated reasons as to why we should
not do this.

First, treating £1 in year 2 as being the same as £1 in year
1 implies that society is indifferent as to when it receives the
£1. But casual reflection will indicate that this is not so. For
by taking the £1 in year 1 we can put it into a savings account
(or some other form of money investment) and earn £1 *plus*
the rate of interest on £1 by year 2. This means that we shall
value £1 in year 1 at *more* than the £1 in year 2. We would
rather have the £1 earlier than later simply because there
exists a positive interest rate in the economy. If we argue
that interest rates exist because of the productivity of capital,
then we have one reason for arguing that a given unit of benefit is worth less the further and further it occurs in the future.

Second, we could simply observe the behaviour of individuals and conclude that, regardless of interest rates, people
do prefer their benefits now rather than later. They could
simply be impatient. Or they might think that, as they will
be richer later on, the £1 in the future will mean less to them.
Hence the earlier the £1 accrues, the more they prefer it. On
either, or both, of these criteria, individuals will have *positive
time preference* − they will prefer now to later.

If we now recall the value judgements underlying our conventional CBA, we observe that the first of these, consumer
sovereignty, dictates that consumer preferences matter. Thus
we cannot logically exclude individuals' preferences about
the incidence of costs and benefits through time. In turn this
means that we must 'discount' future benefits and costs. One
procedure for doing this is indicated by looking at the first

rationale for discounting, the existence of interest rates. £1 in year 1 would accumulate to £$(1 + r)$ in year 2 if the interest rate is r per cent (r is typically expressed as the corresponding decimal – e.g. 5 per cent would be 0.05, 12 per cent would be 0.12, and so on). *Looked at from the standpoint of year 1*, we can ask the question: 'How much is £1 in year 2 worth to us in year 1?' The answer will be that it is worth £$1/(1 + r)$, for the simple reason that if we had this sum in year 1 we could invest it at r per cent and obtain in year 2

$$\frac{£1}{(1 + r)} \times (1 + r) = £1$$

In the same way, we see that £1 in year 3 can be expressed as a value to us in year 1 as follows:

$$£1/(1 + r)^2$$

since in year 3

$$\frac{£1}{(1 + r)^2} \times (1 + r) \times (1 + r) = £1$$

We now have the general formula for discounting. A benefit B in any year t can be written as B_t, and from the above procedure we know that this benefit will have a value to us in year 1 of

$$\frac{B_t}{(1 + r)^t} \tag{4.1}$$

Notice the procedure whereby we look at future benefits (and costs, the procedure is the same) from the standpoint of the present. This is why expressions such as equation (4.1) are called *present values*. The procedure for finding a present value is known as *discounting* and the rate at which the benefits or costs are discounted is known as the *discount rate*. In CBA we are concerned with the costs and benefits to a whole society. Hence the discount rate we use will be a *social discount rate*.

Before proceeding to the sources of the social discount rate it is as well to remove one potential source of misunderstanding. The discount rate has nothing to do with inflation. This is because there is always one adjustment to be made with respect to benefits and costs and this is to ensure that they are expressed in *real terms*, i.e. net of any general movements in price levels. This is done by expressing their values in terms of some base-year set of prices. Since benefits and costs are in real terms, so is the discount rate, to ensure that inflation is not relevant to the determination of the discount rate. In particular, the reasons as to why individuals discount the future are exclusive of any expectations they might have about the rate of inflation. This said, it is sometimes the case that actual CBA studies quote both 'money' and 'real' discount rates. For example, with 7 per cent inflation, a 5 per cent real discount rate is the same as a 12 per cent money rate of discount.

Finding the discount rate

In order to analyse further the foundations of a social discount rate, consider Figure 4.1. This shows consumption in two years, t and $t + 1$. The function TT' is a *transformation function*, or *production possibility curve*, but, instead of the familiar form of alternative configurations of the production of two goods, it shows the possible configurations of production between two *years*. It says, for example, that if resources are wholly devoted to year t, output will be OT. If they are wholly devoted to year $t + 1$ output would be OT'. Notice that OT' is greater than OT. This is intuitively acceptable because devoting resources to production in year $t + 1$ means, given that we have measured the transformation in terms of units of consumpton, that OT' can only come about by investing all the resources that would have been consumed in year t. That is, if the economy is at position T' it means that

OT was invested in year *t* and the consumption goods resulting are *OT′* in year *t* + 1.

Also shown in Figure 4.1 is what looks like an indifference curve. This is a *social* indifference curve indicating the combinations of consumption in period *t* (C_t) and consumption in period *t* + 1 (C_{t+1}) between which society is indifferent. This is denoted by *SS′*.

Clearly, society will be in an optimal position if it located at point *X*, for then society is able at this point to climb on to the highest possible social indifference curve given the constraints set down by the function *TT′*. In fact we can find

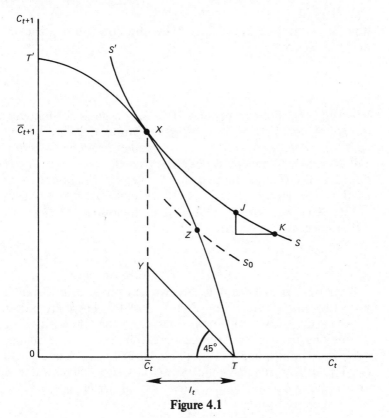

Figure 4.1

out just how much investment and consumption occurs if the economy settles at X. We can read off C_t and C_{t+1} immediately and we see that these are given by $\bar{C}_t$ and $\bar{C}_{t+1}$. But TT' embodies the investment that also takes place, i.e. the difference between $\bar{C}_t$ and OT must be the level of real investment in year t, I_t. In turn we see that it is I_t that generates the consumption level C_{t+1}. Using these ideas we can establish some important equations.

First, observing the level of investment I_t, we can see that

$$\frac{\bar{C}_{t+1}}{I_t} = \frac{Y\bar{C}_t + XY}{I_t} = \frac{Y\bar{C}_t}{I_t} + \frac{XY}{I_t} \qquad (4.2)$$

But $Y\bar{C}_t = I_t$ because $Y\bar{C}_t$ is drawn by constructing the 45° line YT. Hence

$$\frac{\bar{C}_{t+1}}{I_t} = 1 + \frac{XY}{I_t} \qquad (4.3)$$

Note that the first expression in (4.3) is the gross productivity of capital, and XY/I_t is in fact the *net* productivity of capital, or its *internal rate of return* (or *marginal efficiency of capital*). Yet this latter concept is precisely the discount rate introduced as the first of the two alternatives, i.e. the interest rate in the economy, r. Moreover, if we make I_t very small in Figure 4.1, we can see that $\bar{C}_{t+1}/I_t$ measures the *slope* of TT'. Hence we can rewrite (4.3) as

$$\text{Slope of } TT' = 1 + r \qquad (4.4)$$

where r is now the marginal rate of return on capital.

Turning our attention to SS' we can proceed in a similar way. Consider points J and K in Figure 4.1. These are points on the same social indifference curve, so that the utility *lost* by moving from K to J would be $\Delta C_t MU_t$ — i.e. the change ('Δ') in C_t multiplied by the marginal utility associated with C_t. The utility *gained* would be $\Delta C_{t+1} MU_{t+1}$. Since J and K are on the same indifference curve, we can write

$$-\Delta C_t MU_t = \Delta C_{t+1} MU_{t+1} \qquad (4.5)$$

and hence

$$\frac{-\Delta C_{t+1}}{\Delta C_t} = \text{Slope of } SS' = \frac{MU_t}{MU_{t+1}} \tag{4.6}$$

The slope of SS' is simply the ratio of the two marginal utilities of consumption (which is what we would expect from our knowledge of indifference curves in general).

Now, as we move along SS' in the direction J to K, society will tend to require more and more C_{t+1} to compensate for a unit loss of C_t. Very simply, $\Delta C_{t+1}/\Delta C_t > 1$. Hence we now have, from (4.6),

$$\frac{MU_t}{MU_{t+1}} > 1 \tag{4.7}$$

Writing the excess of this ratio over unity as S, we have

$$\frac{MU_t}{MU_{t+1}} = 1 + s = \text{Slope of } SS' \tag{4.8}$$

We now define s as the *social rate of time preference.*

The inequality of the two rates of discount

The preceding section has demonstrated that we have two candidates for the social discount rate. The first is r, which we saw was the marginal net product of capital, or the rate of return, or the marginal efficiency of capital. In the literature on CBA it is also known as the *social opportunity cost of capital*, the idea being that we should calculate r for CBA purposes by looking at the projects that are displaced by any given investment and seeing what rate of return they would have earned. The intuitive logic of this approach is very appealing. To use the rate r for discounting purposes is equivalent to saying that our project in the public sector must do at least as well as the projects it displaces, and these may well be in the private sector.

For example, suppose we are considering investing in a

road project. We have already determined, say, that the rate of return on marginal projects in the private sector is 8 per cent. If we use a discount rate of 8 per cent for our public project and the resulting present value of benefits *minus* costs is negative, i.e. costs exceed benefits when discounted, then what we have said is that the project in question must be rejected because the funds are better diverted to projects in the private sector which can earn 8 per cent.

The second discount rate is s. The problem we have is that s is not observable, at least directly. But suppose we determine that it is 5 per cent. Then we would apply this rate to all public projects because *it represents the rate at which society is prepared to trade present for future consumption*. This social time preference rate is obviously consistent with the value judgement about consumers' sovereignty.

Are r and s likely to diverge? From Figure 4.1 we can see that there is one circumstance in which they will not diverge, namely when the economy is operating at X, which is a (constrained) optimum. If X is an optimal position, then the level of investment, I_t must also be an optimum. And at X the values of r and s are the same because the slopes of TT' and SS' are the same. Hence we conclude that if the level of investment in the economy is optimal, $s = r$ and we have no problem about the selection of the discount rate. We can use either approach, and since r seems eminently more observable than s, it would seem sensible to use r. At X, then, the social time preference rate equals the social opportunity cost of capital. Again, this would seem to be an intuitively sensible result if the capital market operates perfectly since the rate of return obtained on projects in the economy should be equal to the rate of interest savers require, and that rate of interest is in turn determined by individuals' time preference. That is, the forces that determine the real interest rate in the economy are the demand for funds, and this reflects the availability of projects with positive net capital productivity, and the supply of funds, which reflects savers' behaviour.

In practice s does not equal r, and for many reasons. We can consider one simple explanation. If the public sector can borrow at s per cent the private sector of the economy will have to do better than s per cent to attract funds from investors. This is because of the existence of company taxation (corporation tax), which means that if a company is to pay s per cent to its lenders it must in fact *earn* r per cent, where

$$r = \frac{s}{1 - t}$$

and t is the tax rate on companies and is less than unity. For example, if the tax rate is 40 per cent, and s is 10 per cent, then companies must earn

$$\frac{0.1}{1 - 0.4} = 0.167$$

i.e. 16.7 per cent, for them to be able to pay 10 per cent to investors. Hence company taxation necessarily makes r greater than s (Baumol, 1968).

There are other reasons for supposing that s and r diverge. Government projects tend to be 'riskless', not because they are individually subject to less risk than private-sector projects (often the reverse is the case), but the sheer size of the public sector means that the risk per project is small because of the ability to 'pool' risks across many projects, or across the many people who make up society (Arrow and Lind, 1970). If risk in the private sector is positive, then the value of r will be increased to reflect the 'risk premium'. In this way r will diverge even further from s. Last, the value of r reflects decisions made by individuals acting in their own interest. The *relevant* value of s, however, could be argued to be that which society expresses when it considers projects from a 'social standpoint'. That is, acting in isolation of one another, individuals will express one discount rate, but if they know that their decision to invest is going to be associated with the decision of many others to invest they will tend to quote a lower rate of discount (Sen, 1967). Again, the effect is to produce a high r relative to the value of s.

All this suggests that, instead of operating at point X in Figure 4.1, the economy will be operating at a point below X — i.e. somewhere on the section TX, such as Z. But if it is doing this then it is on a lower social indifference curve, such as S_0 as shown. It is thus in a 'second-best' situation. In such a position we can choose from three options:

1. use r and reject s
2. use s and reject r
3. adjust the decision rule for CBA so that both r and s are reflected in the decision.

Each option has its adherents in the literature on CBA. The reasons for using s *or* r have already been given. Accordingly, we confine our attention to the issue of how the decision rule for CBA might reflect *both* s and r. Before doing that we should observe that there is no very clear consensus either of how to compute the value of r and s anyway! Since s is the more complex of the two, the appendix to this chapter indicates a procedure for deriving values of s. The reader should not assume, however, that finding values for r is without its difficulties.

Adjusting the decision rule

The decision rule obtained in Chapter 3 was that benefits should exceed costs before we consider a project to be a candidate for acceptance. This chapter has shown that we need to introduce time and discounting. The formal requirement for potential acceptance, then, is now as follows:

$$\sum_{t=1}^{t=T} \frac{B_t}{(1+r)^t} - \sum_{t=1}^{t=T} \frac{C_t}{(1+r)^t} > 0 \qquad (4.9)$$

where

B_t is the benefit in time t
T is the 'time horizon' — i.e. the period over which benefits and costs are calculated
r is the social opportunity cost rate of discount
Σ means 'sum of'

Note that (4.9) could be rewritten using s instead of r. The expression involving benefits is the present value of benefits, PV (B), and PV (C) is the present value of costs. We can thus write:

$$NPV = PV(B) - PV(C) \qquad (4.10)$$

where NPV reads 'net present value'. Expression (4.9) requires that NPV > 0.

Before looking at ways in which we can try to account for the second-best position in respect of r and s, it is as well to note two alternative formulations of the rule in (4.9) which are common in the CBA literature. Instead of the summation sign Σ, we may find use of the integral sign $\int$. This is convenient when the discount factor $1/(1 + r)^t$ is expressed in terms of 'continuous time' — i.e. we do not break time up into discrete periods such as years. In this case (4.9) would appear as

$$\int_0^T (B_t e^{-rt} - C_t e^{-rt}) > 0 \qquad (4.11)$$

(Notice the use of e^{-rt}, which is the value $e = 2.718 \ldots$, the natural base for logarithms, raised to the power *minus rt*, where r is the discount rate; e^{-rt} is the same as $1/e^{rt}$.)

Particularly convenient for deriving certain results (as we shall see) is the fact that when T is made equal to infinity, so that we calculate benefits and costs over an 'infinite time horizon', then the integrals in equation (4.11) have the values B/r and C/r respectively, so that (4.11) would read:

$$\frac{B}{r} - \frac{C}{r} = \frac{B - C}{r} > 0 \qquad (4.12)$$

Now, we wish to know how the decision rule is affected by an attempt to introduce *both s* and *r* into the analysis. Various approaches have been used to re-express the decision rule in this way. We follow the approach pioneered by Marglin (1963; 1967). A separate approach is that given by Feldstein (1972), but it is possible to demonstrate that, under certain conditions, Feldstein's approach is the same as Marglin's (see Pearce and Nash, 1981). The result obtained in (4.12) above will now prove useful. We shall work with infinite time horizons, which means that our benefits and costs are *perpetuities*. Marglin's approach is generally spoken of as producing a 'synthetic' discount rate. In fact it does not derive a *single* discount rate at all, but adjusts the NPV(*B*) formula in equation (4.9).

The essence of all synthetic approaches is that they differentiate the sources of finance for a project. They may also differentiate types of benefit. Sources may be broadly split between *taxes* and *borrowing*, while benefits may be differentiated according to whether they generate cash flows, which are reinvestable, or benefit flows, which are not. Let benefits be constant at *B* per year; then we have

$$\text{PV (benefits)} = \frac{B}{s} \tag{4.13}$$

given that we are working with perpetuities, and *s*, the social time preference rate, is the 'fundamental' discount rate.

When looking at *costs*, however, we need to consider what proportion of the finance comes from taxes and what from government borrowing. The general argument is that *taxes* are at the expense of forgone consumption so that the cost is measured in consumption units. *Borrowing* is held to be at the expense of forgone private investment. Let the total capital cost be *K* and let it all occur in the very first period, such that

$$K = I + C_0 \tag{4.14}$$

where *I* is forgone private investment and C_0 is forgone consumption. Thus I can be thought of as earning r, and C can be thought of as earning s. In perpetuity and discounting at s we then have

$$K = \frac{Ir}{s} + \frac{Cs}{s} = \frac{Ir}{s} + C_0. \qquad (4.15)$$

The required inequality for potential acceptance of the project is now

$$\frac{B}{s} > \frac{Ir}{s} + C_0 \qquad (4.16)$$

Note that if $C_0 = 0$, we have

$$\frac{B}{s} > \frac{Ir}{s}$$

or

$$\frac{B}{r} > r \qquad (4.17)$$

which, in the simple case under consideration, is a restatement of the social opportunity cost argument.

Now we can consider what happens on the benefit side. For every £1 of benefit flow, assume a fraction b accrues as a reinvestable cash flow and the remainder $(1 - b)$ as a consumption benefit which cannot be reinvested. Then we can write:

$$B(£1) = br + (1 - b) \qquad (4.18)$$

where it will be seen that the reinvestable fraction earns a rate of return r when reinvested. Notice again that if all benefits accrue as non-reinvestable consumption benefits, b equals 0 and £1 of benefit is simple recorded as £1 of benefit. By allowing for reinvestment we have implicitly attached a shadow price to £1 of (nominal) benefits. The benefit side of the equation now reads

$$\frac{B}{s}[b/r + (1 - b)] \tag{4.19}$$

Substituting (4.19) into (4.16) brings both the source of finance and type of benefit issues together. We obtain

$$\frac{B}{s}[b/r + (1 - b)] > \left[\frac{I/r}{s} + C_0\right]$$

or

$$\frac{B}{s} > \frac{I/r + C_0 s}{s[b/r + (1 - b)]} \tag{4.20}$$

Multiplying both sides by s gives

$$B > \frac{I/r + C_0 s}{b/r + (1 - b)} \tag{4.21}$$

Equations (4.20) and (4.21) describe the essence of the synthetic approach. To check its validity, suppose reinvestment possibilities do not exist. In that case $b = 0$, and equation (4.21) will reduce to

$$B > Ir + C_0 s$$

or

$$\frac{B}{s} > \frac{I/r}{s} + C_0 \tag{4.22}$$

which is the same as equation (4.16)

We have now derived a CBA rule which incorporates both s and r. There are problems with the approach which we do not pursue here (see Pearce and Nash, 1981). The approach by Feldstein (1972) can also be demonstrated to fit in with the previous derivation, though once we move from the hypothetical world of perpetuities the formal equivalence breaks down.

Ranking projects

Equation (4.20) gives us a procedure for relating costs to benefits over time. We see that we need to estimate the flow of benefits B and the flow of sacrificed consumption C_0 (note that C_0 is *not* an expression for cost, but instead refers to *consumption*). We also need values for r and s and the fraction, b, of benefits that are likely to be reinvested. Obviously, the use of a 'synthetic' procedure such as that described in the previous section will begin to impose formidable informational difficulties. Largely for this reason, but also because argument about the use of 'synthetic' procedures still goes on, most CBA studies make use of the more simple approach given in equation (4.9) using either r or s as the discount rate. We revert to that simple procedure in order to demonstrate a proposition we have so far only hinted at.

The requirement that B be greater than C is not sufficient for us to sanction investment in the project in question. We can say that $B > C$ is a *necessary* condition for approval, but it is not *sufficient*. This is because we shall invariably face a limited budget and we cannot undertake all projects where B exceeds C. We therefore require a ranking procedure. It is tempting simply to rank by the value of NPV(B). But this is actually mistaken.

This is easily seen by looking at Table 4.1. This shows three projects, X, Y and Z, with their present value of their

Table 4.1

Project	PV(C)	PV(B)	NPV(B)	PV(B) ÷ PV(C)
X	100	200	100	2.0
Y	50	110	60	2.2
Z	50	120	70	2.4

benefits, costs and net benefits. Suppose the budget constraint is 100 units. Then a ranking by NPV(B) would suggest
X, Z, Y and we would undertake X only with a cost of 100.
The gain to society would be NPY(X) = 100. But casual
inspection shows that we could afford Y and Z, and the NPV
would be NPV(Y) + NPV(Z) = 60 + 70 = 130. Clearly ranking
by NPV does not give us the right answer. This is given by a
ranking of PV(B) *divided by* PV(C), or the so-called *benefit–
cost ratio*.

Discounting and future generations

Regardless of how we derive a discount rate, it it likely to
produce a positive value. Suppose now that the project in
question has benefits that accrue for thirty years but costs
which, while small each year, accrue for 500 years. This
might typify, say, the problem of investing in the safe storage
of nuclear fuel waste and other wastes from nuclear power
stations. The problem, in CBA terms, would present itself as
comparing the costs of the storage system (say placing the
waste in glassified blocks, inside metal containers and then
locating them in depositories deep underground) with the
benefits in terms of the reduced risk of exposure to radio-
activity. Clearly, the more we spend on the storage system,
the lower the risks are likely to be. But let us suppose that
we can never quite get to absolute certainty that no adverse
consequence will occur. We then have (probabilistic) costs
over a long period of time and 500 years is a quite reasonable
estimate of how long we would wish to exercise control over
the storage system, provided of course that we care for future
generations. If we engage in conventional CBA we shall discount the benefits and costs. We can now highlight a problem.
Suppose that the event of an accident is known to us with
certainty and that it occurs in year 500 after we begin
storing the waste. Let us be somewhat more heroic and
suppose that we also know what the cost will be if such an

52

accident occurred, and we set it at £10 billion at today's prices. Our discounting formula requires us to estimate the present value of the cost of the accident at

$$\frac{£10 \text{ billion}}{(1 + r)^{500}}$$

Suppose r is 5 per cent. Then we need to calculate the 'discount factor' $1/(1.05)^{500}$. Reference to the logarithm tables will show us that this is the reciprocal of 3.9×10^{10}. Hence the present value of the accident cost is

$$\frac{£10^9 \times 10}{3.9 \times 10^{10}} = \frac{1}{3.9} = £0.25$$

The £10 billion accident has a cost of only 25 pence in present value terms!

While the example may be thought to be an extreme one, it illustrates a basic problem with CBA, namely that the effect of discounting is to discriminate against the future. Various views can be taken about this. There are those who argue that we cannot take account of costs to generations yet unborn, for to do so is to widen the concept of 'democratic voting' in an unacceptable way. Those who are alive at the time of the decision constitute the 'proper' electorate. Others draw attention to the fact that the kind of 'intergenerational discrimination' implicit in discounting is an increasing feature of our society. Examples might be the potential for heating up the atmosphere through continued burning of fossil fuels (the 'greenhouse effect'), nuclear power waste problems, continued and expanding use of toxic metals and chemicals which do not degrade in the environment, the use of chloro-fluorocarbons (CFCs) which punch 'holes' in the stratosphere and increase the amount of ultra-violet rays in certain areas, perhaps inducing skin cancers, and so on.

It seems fair to say that there is no consensus at all on what to do about this aspect of CBA. Elsewhere I (Pearce, 1983) have drawn attention to the fact that, whatever the ethical basis we use for CBA, the discrimination problem is overcome if we can set up an 'intergenerational compensation fund'. This would simply apply the Kaldor–Hicks criterion through time but with *actual* compensation occurring. Suppose, for example, that we believe the cost to future generations in year 100 will be £1 billion. In order to overcome the discrimination we set aside a compensation fund in year 1. If the interest rate is 5 per cent (notice this need not be the same as the social discount rate – we are interested in investing in a compound interest fund so that only *actual* interest rates are relevant), then we know that we can set aside

$$\frac{£1 \text{ billion}}{(1.05)^{100}}$$

in year 1 and this will grow at 5 per cent for 100 years to become

$$\frac{£1 \text{ billion}}{(1.05)^{100}} \times (1.05)^{100} = £1 \text{ billion}$$

in year 100. More generally, if the anticipated cost is C_t in year t, then we need to set aside

$$X = C_t e^{-rt}$$

as a compensation fund.

The problems with this approach are fairly obvious. We may not know when the cost will occur, nor the size of it, nor can we be sure that the value of r will be constant for 100 years (indeed, we can be sure it won't be!). But uncertainty is a fact of life, and while the compensation fund concept is open to considerable practical difficulties it is perhaps worth pursuing. We may note that many cost–benefit analysts would argue that such a fund is not needed anyway. They would say that future generations are already compensated by the fact that the project in question will add to the capital stock of the nation and hence to future capabilities to invest in solutions to any problems 'shifted' on to them by current generations and to invest in welfare-improving activities. It is perhaps this argument that distinguishes the intergenerational 'hardliners' from those who would set a constraint on CBA to the effect that no investment takes place if it constrains the choices of future generations. Space forbids a detailed treatment, and the reader is referred to some of the excellent contributions to these issues (Page, 1977; Goodin, 1982; Barry, 1982).

Appendix: deriving a social time preference rate

Typically, cost—benefit analysts adopt a discount rate for marginal income of greater than zero, at least partly because the group of persons making decisions about future costs and benefits comprise the current generation. The current generation may exhibit concern for future generations, but that concern is not 'wholly altruistic'. As we have seen, a discount rate for public-sector decision-making can be obtained by:

1. adoption of a direct estimate of a (social) time preference rate, *or*
2. adoption of a direct estimate of an opportunity cost rate *or*
3. some mixture of both.

The foregoing discount rates are generally referred to as 'efficiency' rates because they have a close relationship to the economist's concept of an efficient allocation of resources both within any time period and through time. They apply to income, and it is often argued that the corresponding discount rate for *utility* is lower. This is because with economic growth people in future will be richer and may suffer less from a given small decrease in their income and conversely be willing to pay more for a given increase in utility. However, efficiency rates of this kind virtually always include the judgement that the current generation's preferences shall dominate. If this judgement is changed so that marginal utility to future generations is placed on an *equal* basis ('pure altruism') with damage to current generations, then the relevant discount rate for *utility* becomes zero.

A change in income leads to a change in welfare or general well-being or 'utility'. The source of this utility is consumption, which is proportional to income. A typical assumption is that the consumption—utility function has the form

$$U = U(C) \tag{4.23}$$

where

$$\frac{dU}{dc} = U' = aC^b \tag{4.24}$$

and a and b are constants. U' is the marginal utility of consumption —i.e. the extra utility arising from an extra unit of consumption — and this exhibits a *declining* level as dC increases (i.e. b is negative). Now, if consumption can be expected to grow through time, dU/dC will have a different value at time t than now ($t = 0$). Thus $U'_t = aC_0^b$ and $U'_0 = aC_0^b$. The weight to be given to marginal consumption in period t is then

$$w_t = \frac{U'_t}{U'_t} = \frac{aC_t^b}{aC_0^b} = \frac{C_t^b}{C_0} = (1 + c)^{bt} \tag{4.25}$$

where c is the annual rate of growth of consumption per head through time. The value of c is something that can be directly estimated. The value of b is not observable but has generally been regarded, on indirect evidence, as having a value of -1 to -2. Moreover, the measure of consumption that is relevant is *consumption per capita* – otherwise we would have a situation in which individual welfare rises simply because more people have the same average level of consumption. Hence the growth rate 'c' can be decomposed into two parts – the growth rate of total consumption, k, and the growth rate of population, π. Equation (4.25) would then become

$$w_t = \left(\frac{1 + k}{1 + \pi}\right)^b \tag{4.26}$$

In turn, w_t can be expressed as a discount rate, r, in the following manner:

$$w_t = \frac{1}{(1+r)^t} = \left(\frac{1+k}{1+\pi}\right)^{bt} \qquad (4.27)$$

From (4.27) we have

$$(1+r)^t = \left(\frac{1+\pi}{1+k}\right)^{bt}$$

Therefore,

$$1+r = \left(\frac{1+\pi}{1+k}\right)^{b}$$

Therefore

$$r = \left(\frac{1+k}{1+\pi}\right)^{-b} - 1 \qquad (4.28)$$

Now, it is also possible to discount *utility*, and some writers (e.g. Olson and Bailey, 1981) reserve the term 'positive time preference' for utility discounting alone. If we now discount utility at a rate p, we shall modify equation (4.28) to

$$\bar{w}_t = \frac{1}{1+\bar{r}} = \frac{1}{1+p} \times \left(\frac{1+k}{1+\pi}\right)^{b} \qquad (4.29)$$

where $\bar{w}$ and $\bar{r}$ indicate a modified w and r, and $\bar{r}$ is a social time preference rate which discounts income first because of its declining marginal utility (giving equation (4.28), and then additionally because of positive time preference.

Setting

$$1 + \bar{r} = e^{\bar{r}} = \underline{r}$$

$$1 + p = e^{p} = \underline{p}$$

$$1 + k = e^{k} = \underline{k}$$

$$1 + \pi = e^{\pi} = \underline{\pi}$$

and modifying (4.29) to read

$$1 + \bar{r} = \left(\frac{1+\pi}{1+k}\right)^b \times (1 + p) \tag{4.30}$$

we have

$$\bar{r} = \underline{\pi}b - \underline{k}b + \underline{p}$$
$$= \underline{\pi}b - (\underline{c} + \underline{\pi})b + \underline{p}$$
$$= \underline{p} - \underline{c}b \tag{4.31}$$

Thus the discount rate for consumption, and hence for income, is made up of the positive time preference rate (p), and the growth rate of consumption (c) and the marginal utility of income (b) (b is negative, so the two discount rates are added). There is 'hard' evidence on c, a sort of consensus on b, while the estimate of p will have to be purely judgemental. If we adopt the 'pure altruism' approach, p vanishes and only c and b are relevant. Table 4.2 shows a range of discount rates that emerge from the analysis assuming economic growth such that $c = 2$.

Table 4.2

p	$\bar{r}$ for values of:		
	$\underline{c} = 2, b = -1$	$\underline{c} = 2, b = -1.5$	$\underline{c} = 2, b = -2$
0	2	3	4
1	3	4	5
2	4	5	6

Some final brief comments are worth making about this derivation of the social discount rate. If we reject utility discounting on the grounds that it is irrational (Ramsey, 1928; Pigou, 1952), then $p = 0$ and the discount rate is determined by cb alone. But the expectation that c will continue to be positive (for long periods of time) could be false. Perhaps future real incomes will decline or simply stay constant. If so, $c = 0$ and the discount rate will become zero. It is possible, then, to get to the 'altruistic' discount rate of zero without engaging in ethical arguments about the rights of future generations.

5

Efficiency and Distributive Weights

Chapter 1 indicated that there are two fundamental normative judgements underlying what we might term 'conventional' CBA which we have formalised in terms of the net benefit criterion in Chapters 3 and 4. These judgements were (a) that consumer preferences count, and (b) that the existing distribution of income is, in some sense, 'optimal'. We now need to investigate this second judgement more closely.

Imagine that society consists of four individuals, A, B, C, and D. We can for the moment ignore time (and hence the discount rate). Let A, B and C each gain £100 from a project, but D loses £200. Our CBA formula tells us that the sum of the benefits is £300 and the sum of the losses is £200, so there is a net benefit of £100. The project is potentially worth while. We could write the net benefit calculation as follows:

$$\text{Net benefit} = a_A B_A + a_B B_B + a_C B_C - a_D B_D$$

where B_A, is the benefit to A, ... The introduction of the 'weights' a_A, a_B, etc., serves to underline an important feature of conventional CBA. This is that it sets a weight of *unity* to each £1 of benefit (or cost) regardless of who receives that benefit or who suffers the cost. This is essentially what we mean by saying that conventional CBA adopts the second value judgement, namely that the income distribution is optimal. To emphasise the point, the fact that D could be very poor and A, B and C all equally rich is immaterial for conventional CBA.

It is this kind of consideration which has led to the emergence within the CBA literature of a school of thought which seeks to *vary* the weights a_A, etc. Typically it will do this in such a way that, given the statements about the comparative incomes of $A, \ldots, D$ in our example, it will make a_D greater than $a_A, \ldots, A_C$. Now, within this school of thought, dubbed 'revisionist' by Mishan (1982), there are two sub-schools. One would argue that the numerical values of the weights $a_A, \ldots,$ a_D are determined by reference to the political system. That is, one would look to the decision-maker's objectives and derive from them a set of weights, *and* only one set. In this respect the weights become shadow prices just like any other shadow price such as the price to be used for labour, the social discount rate, and so on. Examples of this kind of approach can be found in Little and Mirrlees (1974) and Marglin, Sen and Dasgupta (1972). It seems fair to say that this approach has found its major use in projected appraisal in less developed countries. The other sub-school of the revisionists would argue that, while derivation of weights from overt statements by politicians is not ruled out, it is open to the analyst himself to indicate the way in which the results of the CBA vary with differing judgements on the weights. For this approach, then, there will be *several* sets of results, and the prodcedure has been called 'value sensitivity analysis' by Nash, Pearce and Stanley (1975).

Conventional CBA *vs* 'revisionism'

There are many objections to the use of these distributional weights, and they have been forcefully expressed by Mishan (1974; 1981; 1982). We can deal with some general ones before developing procedures for deriving the weights, after which we can consider some more detailed objections. The first objection is, effectively, that while conventional CBA proceeds *as if* the existing distribution of income is optimal, it is always open to government to adjust the distribution of income by wholly separate means, e.g. by making lump-sum transfers from gainers to losers in just the way that the Kaldor–Hicks test *hypothesises* (recall that the application of the test does not require the *actual* transfer of money). Effectively, then, we could argue that while CBA itself proceeds on the basis of the optimality of the existing income distribution, government itself can ameliorate the effects of any decision through a wholly separate income transfer between affected parties. An additional reason for supporting this view is that cited by Mishan (1974) to the effect that any weighting procedure will still be consistent with making the rich richer and the poor poorer. For example, if we selected, by some procedure, the weights

$$a_A, a_B, a_C = 0.7; \text{ and } a_D = 1.0$$

in our numerical example, it will then be the case that recorded benefits will be 210 and costs 200. The project is still worth while even though *D* is the poorest. But if weighting is consistent with making the rich richer and the poor poorer, what is the point of the procedure?

The 'revisionist' answer to these objections would be along the following lines. First, one of the reasons that the Kaldor–Hicks test deals in hypothetical as opposed to actual compensation is precisely because of the complexities of making lump-sum transfers. Fiscal measures are influenced by many factors and it is simply not the case that they are better suited to 'correcting' the distribution of income than via the use of project selection (Pearce and Nash, 1981, p. 30). Second, to say that weighting procedures are consistent with continuing to make the rich richer is to miss the point. It implies that the *purpose* of weighting is actually to improve the distribution of income *regardless of the conventional measure of efficiency*. But this has never been the aim of the revisionist schools of thought. For the weighting procedures used deliberately 'mix' efficiency and distributional features. In that respect it is not at all surprising that we can construct examples in which projects are selected but in which the distribution is made worse. All this means is that the distributional weights do not outbalance the efficiency effects. To make the argument crystal clear, if we were concerned *never* to make the distribution of income worse, then we would always select weights to ensure that this was the case. In our numerical example it is simple to find the requisite weight to achieve this. We calculate the ration of losses to benefits (i.e. 200/300) to get the weight 0.666. Applying this to the benefits we obtain the result that any weight *less* than 0.666 will achieve the result that the project is rejected because of its effects on D, the poorest. This is equivalent to adopting a Rawls-type social criterion whereby we always seek to make the poorest group better off (Rawls, 1972). But while this is one social decision rule, it happens not to be one advocated by the revisionists. We conclude that Mishan has misunderstood the purpose of the revisionist exercise, which is to *integrate* efficiency and distribution.

Now, having established the function of weighting procedures we need to consider Mishan's next objection, which is that the values of a_A, etc., are 'arbitrary'. Here, again, the objection is not sustainable. In the case of 'politically determined' weights, the procedure for deriving them is by reference to some social objective function, albeit laid down by a political authority. Such a procedure is not arbitrary – it derives directly from a given objective function. In the case of the second group of revisionists, the charge of arbitrariness is more telling, because we have not as yet determined any rules for selecting the weights. Instead of 'several' results in a value sensitivity test, then, we could have a great many. Mishan's criticism should thus be treated as a caution against proliferating such weights. We shall suggest below various criteria for selecting weights. But it is worth noting that the adoption of a set of weights equal to *unity* is itself arbitrary *unless* the distribution of income is held to be optimal. This observation holds regardless of whether lump-sum transfers are possible. We argue, then, that it is conventional CBA which is either arbitrary in its selection of weights, or that conventional CBA implies the value judgement about the optimality of the distribution of income.

Before proceeding to the derivation of weights, we may consider a further objection by Mishan, namely that the weights chosen are not independent of political authority. Moreover, because of this, they will vary from one country to another and from one year to another as political authorities change within any one country. As Mishan (1982) states, 'what is presented as an economic calculation has, in fact, no meaning or sanction independent of the will of the relevant political authority'. If this is true at all, it is true only of the 'unique-weight' theorists among the revisionists. The objection does not hold for the 'sensitivity analysts'. In their case, some of the weights may come from the political authority but none need in fact do so. However, if they do come from a political authority, it is surely no surprise that the weights will vary with changes in that authority. After all, the implicit prices placed on a great many things change when governments change. A government wedded to more 'law and order' places a greater value, 'on behalf' of society, on the rights to life, limb and property than those who might prefer a lower police profile in the interests of protecting the freedoms of the individual. Effectively, the 'relative prices' of civil liberties and individuals' assets change. Mishan's objection only really holds in the sense that he sees an objection to the *subservience* of the economist to political authority. Here we must surely have sympathy with his viewpoint, and for this reason we do not wholly subscribe to the unique-weighting school of thought. In its defence, however, it is worth noting that this school of thought has its main application in less developed countries where the economy often is very closely planned. In such a circumstance it *is* the objective function of the political authority that matters.

Deriving distributional weights

Now we can consider ways in which weights other than unity might be obtained. First, consider the difference between political and economic votes that was alluded to in Chapter 1. There it was noted that a political vote is not (generally) 'weighted' by an intensity of preference, i.e. we have 'one man, one vote'. Economic votes are weighted by income (and wealth). Since the principle of 'one man, one vote' is deeply embedded in the concept of democracy, one weighting procedure for CBA would be to adjust each economic vote so that it accorded with what each person *would* vote if their incomes were equalised. A crude procedure for achieving this result is as follows. We set

$$a_i = \frac{\overline{Y}}{Y_i}$$

where a_i is now the weight to be attached to the ith income group, $\overline{Y}$ is the average income (of the nation, community, etc.) and Y_i is the income of the ith group. Table 5.1 sets out a very simple example of such a weighting procedure. Assuming each group has the same number of persons in it, we see that the average income is 150. This explains the row showing the values of a_i.

We see from Table 5.1 that what would have been a sanctioned project on the conventional CBA procedure is now rejected on the 'revisionist' approach. We can generalise the formula for the new approach as

$$NSB = \sum_i a_i (B_i - C_i)$$

$$(5.2)$$

Table 5.1

Group	A	B	C	D	Net benefit
Y_i	200	250	100	50	
B_i	+100	+100	+100	−100	+200
a_i	0.75	0.60	1.50	3.00	
a_iB_i	+75	+60	+150	−300	−15

where NSB refers to net social benefit, i refers to the ith income group, and a_i has the meaning given to it in equation (5.1). In terms of the CBA decision rule incorporating time and discounting, the new expression looks a little formidable, and is

$$NSB = \sum_t \sum_i \frac{a_i \, (B_{it} - C_{it})}{(1 + r)^t} \tag{5.3}$$

where r is the social discount rate, and could be either the social time preference rate, or the social opportunity cost rate.

The problem with using equation (5.1) is that a hypothetical change of income from Y_i to $\overline{Y}$ would in fact be accompanied by a change in the individual's expenditure pattern, determined by the income elasticity of demand for the goods in question. To put it another way, equation (5.1) fulfils our requirement of approximating each individual's 'income-equalised' willingness to pay if, and only if, the income elasticity of demand is unity. In a situation in which the elasticity is not unity, the proper formula would be

$$a_i = \left(\frac{\overline{Y}}{Y_i} \right)^b \tag{5.4}$$

65

where b is now the income elasticity of demand. Equation (5.1) then becomes a special case of equation (5.4) in which $b = 1$. (For more detail see Nash, Pearce and Stanley, 1975, and appendix 1 to this chapter.)

We now have a perfectly general formula for weighting costs and benefits. But observe that it is based on the idea of weights as means of approximating economic votes to the 'one man, one vote' principle. It has nothing to do with what is or is not 'deserved' by each of the groups in question. If we wish to adjust for this, either by way of illustration by the analyst to the decision-maker, or through adoption of political judgements about what is socially desirable, then we can introduce a new formula, which would appear as

$$a_i' = \left(\frac{\overline{Y}}{Y_i}\right)^v$$

(5.5)

where v is now some judgemental weighting about 'deservingness'. Indeed, the two procedures in equations (5.4) and (5.5) could be combined to give

$$a_i'' = \left(\frac{\overline{Y}}{Y_i}\right)^{b+v}$$

5.6)

Equation (5.6) is then equivalent to adjusting the 'equalised' votes again for a factor reflecting deservingness, or need, or merit, or whatever.

Problems with weighting procedures

So far we have seen that weights can be derived either using criteria based on 'equalised' votes, or through explicit adoption of politically determined valuations of one group compared with others, or through a combination of both. With Mishan, we would argue that the adoption of the 'v'-type weights should not be undertaken unless there is good reason, or should only be carried out to illustrate for decision-makers

what the 'sensitivity' of the results of a CBA will be to differing judgements. The adoption of income-elasticity weights
does not, however, rest on anything except an attempt to
adjust for the fact that economic votes reflect the existing
distribution of income. Hence 'b'-type weights are not
subject to Mishan's criticism about loss of independence by
the economist.

Given the above derivations, we can now consider other
criticisms made by Mishan. In the formulae given above the
value of *b* was used in order to 'equalise' votes. The basis for
this weighting procedure, then, is based on the value judgement that market votes are unfair. The 'b' weighting approach
is thus ethically derived and the ethical criterion used may or
may not appeal, any more than the use of weights of unity in
conventional CBA may appeal. The value of 'v' could be
politically derived. We have considered Mishan's objections
to politically derived weights and we have argued they are
not wholly valid. But Mishan also objects to 'ethico' weights,
i.e. weights derived from some moral principle. Within this
category he includes weights which reflect the marginal
utility of income to the various individuals. Note that we
have not used this approach at all to derive equations (5.4)
and (5.5). But we could have done. The argument would be
that a benefit of £1 to a rich person is worth less to him than
£1 is to a pauper. If our objective is to maximise the aggregate (cardinal) utility of society, then we would simply set
a_i equal to the marginal utility of income of the *i*th individual, and so on. In effect, the weights will become the ratios
of the marginal utilities so long as we set one of the absolute
weights equal to unity. Appendix 2 to this chapter explains
how marginal utility weights would be obtained. The effect is
to obtain a set of weights where

$$a_i = \left(\frac{\overline{Y}}{Y_i} \right)^{-e} \tag{5.7}$$

where the weight is related to the average income level (but need not be) and *e* is the elasticity of the marginal utility of income function.

Now, the objections to such a procedure are several. We may note that there exists a dispute as to whether the marginal utility of income is observable or measurable at all. If it is not, then there is little point in pursuing adjustments of the kind given in equation (5.7). If it is measurable, then what we have is to convert the CBA formula into one which operates with cardinal – i.e. completely measurable – utility. Mishan's objection to this is that such weights 'have no social sanction whatever'. They are not ethical weights because 'in order to qualify as ethical, the set of weights has to be enshrined in the constitution or else conform with a virtual constitution, one that effectively represents an ethical consensus' (Mishan, 1982, p. 38). Mishan's argument is thus that the conventional CBA approach, in which the weights are set equal to unity, does have such an ethical consensus. Mishan is surely right to observe that society offers little by way of confirmation that maximising aggregate (cardinal) utility is the objective of society. Equally, it is very hard to believe that society approves of the existing distribution of income and has no wish to change it. Mishan's objection is thus equally valid against his own preferred approach. For our purposes we need only observe that 'reasonable' (i.e. likely to command consensus) procedures for weighting need not involve the use of marginal utility of income weights at all, as equations (5.4) and (5.5) show.

Other weighting approaches

We conclude that not only has no case been made against explicit weighting, but that arguments about 'consensus' are very likely to lead us to adopt procedures such as those given in equations (5.4) and (5.5). Other weighting procedures have been proposed. Weisbrod (1966) observes the weights implicit in past government decisions. Assuming that governments actually do make conscious trade-offs between efficiency benefits and other objectives, detailed scrutiny of past decisions may permit derivation of the trade-off ratios, i.e. the weights which reflect social preferences concerning distribution. This general approach has attracted the support of Maass (1966) and empirical studies have been made by Weisbrod (1966) and McGuire and Garn (1969). Weisbrod analysed decisions affecting various income and race groups, and his general results indicated a high relative weight of +9.3 for low-income non-white families, with the remaining weights being +2.2 for higher-income white families, −1.3 for low-income white families and −2.0 for high-income non-whites. If the results can be accepted at all, they indicate a high propensity to favour low-income non-white groups, but thereafter a peculiar ranking in which high-income white families are favoured above low-income white families.

There is clearly room for refinements to this type of approach. At the very least, they indicate to the decision-maker the weights implicit in past decisions, providing 'a general check against absurdities' (McGuire and Garn, 1969). The problems are that *ex post* distributional results may not indicate *ex ante* government plans. Bonnen (1966) has shown that programmes designed to aid low-income farmers in fact produced the opposite effect. In this case the observation of *ex post* weights should at least indicate to the decision-maker that the welfare effects of policies are not precisely predictable. More important, they should assist the decision-maker in becoming more conscious of distributional outcomes.

A variant on the implicit-weights approach involves the use of marginal rates of taxation as weights (Krutilla and Eckstein, 1958). Since the marginal rate tends to rise as income rises, it would seem that society has implicitly assigned lower weights to gains to high-income groups than to low-income groups. The analysis could be generalised to incorporate other allowances; thus family allowances could be argued to reflect society's value weight for families with several children whose effective income is not so high as that for families with the same nominal income but without children. The marginal rate of tax can be converted into a surrogate for the marginal utility of income. The relevant a_i would simply be the inverses of the marginal tax rates. A rate of 25p in the £ would mean a relative weight of 4. As income rises, and the marginal rate rises to, say, 50p in the £, the wieght will fall to 2. The problems with this approach are several. First, tax rates do not reflect only society's set of value judgements concerning equality; they also reflect past decisions of fiscal policy designed to affect the overall level of income. Second, it presumes that only some taxes reflect equity judgements. But indirect taxes may also partly serve this purpose. A full assessment of weights might therefore require an analysis of the true incidence of the entire tax system. In general it would be a stretch of the imagination to suppose that the tax system reflected only equity judgements. In practive it reflects a hotchpotch of influences, not all of which are consistent with the equity argument. Additionally, using observed rates of tax incidence to reflect planners' intentions suffers the same problem noted earlier with Weisbrod's approach.

Conclusions

The approach presented in this chapter is what Mishan has termed 'revisionist', i.e. it argues that there is no single correct approach to CBA. Instead, there are several sets of results depending not only on varying particular values of things such as the discount rate (if this is not the subject of consensus) but also on varying the judgements that may be made about differing weights to be attached to costs and benefits according to *who* benefits and suffers. The practical problem with approaches which do not set weights equal to unity is the additional information required. This, more than appeals to the independence of the economist and the credibility of cost—benefit analysts, is the main reason for not pursuing explicitly weighted procedures. An actual example of a weighted CBA (which uses marginal utility of income weights) is to be found in Pearce and Wise (1972), which corrects a set of erroneous weighted results given earlier by Nwaneri (1970).

Appendix 1: deriving an income-elasticity weighted cost—benefit function

Given a demand curve with the form

$$Q = kY^b P^g \tag{5.8}$$

then the compensating variation for the ith individual is

$$CV_i = \int_{P_1}^{P_2} kY^b P^g dp \tag{5.9}$$

where P_1 and P_2 are the prices after and before the project in question (the lower and upper limits of integration). Similarly, the compensating variation at the average level of income will be

$$CV_Y = \int_{P_1}^{P_2} kY^b P^g dp \tag{5.10}$$

Hence,

$$\frac{CV_{\bar{Y}}}{CV_i} = \left(\frac{\bar{Y}}{Y}\right)^b \tag{5.11}$$

which is equation (5.4) in the text of Chapter 5.

Appendix 2: deriving a marginal utility of income weighting procedure for CBA

Let utility be related to income, i.e. $U = U(Y)$, such that the marginal utility of income function has a constant elasticity. The marginal utility of income function for individual i can then be written

$$U_i' = \frac{dU}{dY_i} = aY_i^{-e} \tag{5.12}$$

where $-e$ is now the elasticity of the function. For the average income $\bar{Y}$, we shall therefore have

$$\frac{U'}{Y} = a\,\bar{Y}^{-e} \tag{5.13}$$

and the relative weight for the ith individual would then be

$$\frac{U'}{Y} = \frac{a\bar{Y}^{-e}}{aY_i^{-e}}\left(= \frac{\bar{Y}}{Y_i}\right)^{-e} \tag{5.14}$$

Notationally (5.14) is similar to (5.11), but the income elasticity of demand in (5.11) is replaced by the elasticity of the marginal utility of income function.

6

Risk and Uncertainty

In the basic cost—benefit formulae presented so far we have assumed that the costs and benefits are known with certainty. In practice, this will not be true, and we can distinguish two situations. The first is in the context of *risk* in which we will know the probability that the benefit or cost will take on particular values. For example, a cost in a given year may be 100, 200, 500 or even 1,000. To each of these values we can attach a probability, say 0.2, 0.5, 0.2 and 0.1 respectively. This means that we judge there is a 20 per cent chance of the cost being 200, a 50 per cent chance of it being 200, and so on. We thus define a risk context as one in which the *probability distribution* is known. The second context is one in which we do not know the probabilities attached to the sizes of the costs or benefits, but in which we do know the values that the costs and benefits could take. In this case we would know, for example, that the cost in a given year is 100, 200, 500 or 1,000, but we do not know what probabilities to attach to each of these possibilities. This context is defined as one of *uncertainty*. In the literature, risk and uncertainty are often used interchangeably, but it is convenient to keep them

73

separate as often as we can. As we shall see, the techniques for dealing with the two different contexts are themselves different.

Risk

The information in our simple example above can be presented diagrammatically in Figure 6.1. The vertical axis shows the probability and the horizontal axis shows the size of the benefit. (We choose to work with the example of benefit – it must be recalled that costs are also likely to be probabilistic.) We can then plot the various possibilities on the diagram as shown. Now, it may well be that the points shown are all the information we have. If so, we are said to possess a *discrete* probability function. Or it may be that we know more than this and that we are able to draw the *continuous probability distribution* as illustrated by the dashed curve in Figure 6.1. In practice, we usually do not know the whole curve, though in some circumstances, such as flood damage and pollution, we can often use a probability distribution obtained from various 'simulations' of how floodwaters or pollution are spread through a given system. These results come from special mathematical and physical models. When probabilities are obtained either from past experience of similar projects or events, or when they come from models of the kind described, they are called *objective probabilities*. But it may often be necessary to rely on judgements about the probabilities, and these are known as *subjective probabilities* since they do not derive from objective data but from assessments by the analyst or some expert. Obviously, quite often, the probabilities will be a mixture of both subjective and objective elements. For our purposes we shall not make the distinction between subjective and objective probabilities again since our treatment of probability will be the same regardless of which type of probability we are dealing with.

Now, we obviously cannot leave the information in Figure

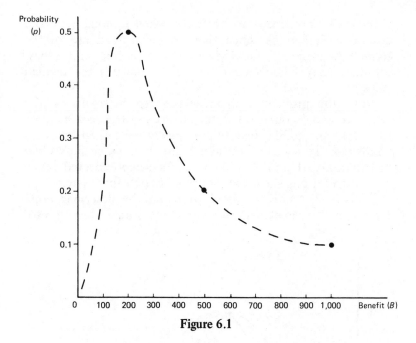

Figure 6.1

6.1 as it is. We need to compress the information as best we can into a single indicator which we can then put into our cost—benefit formula. One fairly obvious way of doing this presents itself immediately. This is to take some sort of *average* from the distribution. In our example the average could be taken as

(0.2 x 100) + (0.5 x 200) + (0.2 x 500)

+ (0.1 x 1,000) = 320

The figure that we would put into the CBA is then 320 and this is the *mean* or *expected value*. Note that the mean or expected value is *not* the same thing as the 'most likely' value of the benefit. Clearly the value that has the highest probability of occurring is 200, with a probability of 0.5. But this is not the expected value. (The value of 200 is the *mode* of the distribution.) Care needs to be taken when looking at actual cost–benefit studies, since there is widespread use of the term 'best estimate' for a given benefit or cost, and a 'best estimate' may be the mean, the mode or even the median value.

Now, the problem with using the expected value as the figure to put in our CBA is that it does not reflect the attitude that the public investment agency concerned takes towards *risk*. To see this consider Figure 6.2, which shows two distributions, *A* and *B*, each with the same expected value. The distributions shown are normal distributions. The reason for this is that normal distributions can be described completely by their expected values and a measure of their 'spread'

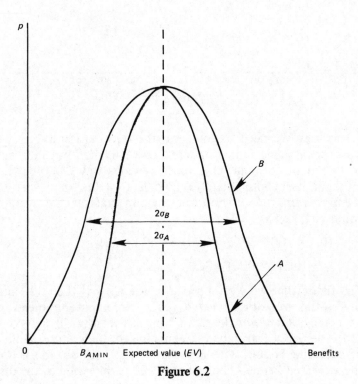

Figure 6.2

or *variance*. Non-normal distributions require further measures, particularly of their 'skewness'. As we shall see, there are problems enough dealing with normal distributions. For this reason studies which do contain probability functions usually attempt to approximate them with normal distributions.

It would be surprising if society were indifferent between the two distributions in Figure 6.2 even though they both have the same expected values. For example, distribution A has as its lowest possible value of benefits $B_{A\ MIN}$, whereas distribution B has a lowest possible value of zero. We would expect society to take account of the greater variance in distribution B. Such a reaction is said to be one of *risk-aversion*. If society were indifferent between the two distributions, i.e. it reacts only to the expected values, then it is *risk-neutral*. We omit consideration of a situation in which there is a positive attitude to large gambles, known as risk-loving.

Since the expected-value approach does not capture risk-aversion, and since we assume society is generally risk-averse, we can approach the problem by saying that the *utility* which society attaches to the various outcomes is the relevant entity, not the size of the outcome on its own. This is sufficient to enable us to restate the problem. Whereas the expected-value approach would have given us

$$EV = p_1 B_1 + p_2 B_2 + \ldots + p_n B_n = \sum_i p_i B_i \tag{6.1}$$

the *expected utility* can be written

$$EU = p_i U(B_1) + p_2 U(B_2) + \ldots + p_n U(B_n)$$

$$= \sum_i p_i U(B_i) \tag{6.2}$$

But we can proceed no further along this line of reasoning unless we know something about the way in which utility and benefits are related – i.e. something about the utility–benefit function.

Typically, such a function is assumed to take on the shape shown in Figure 6.3, i.e. it exhibits diminishing marginal utility as B increases. We can use this function to derive a value of B which we can use in our CBA. We proceed as follows.

Let B_1 and B_2 be the only possible outcomes of our project. Imagine that B_1 is certain. In that case $p_1 = 1$, and $p_2 = 0$. The value of EU will be given by

$$1 \times U(B_1) + 0 \times U(B_2) = U(B_1)$$

which is shown on the vertical axis. Similarly, if B_2 were certain, the same analysis would give us the point $U(B_2)$.

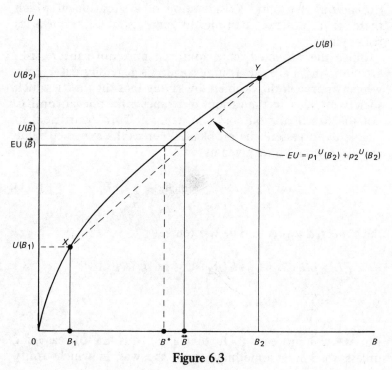

Figure 6.3

This exercise enables us to fix the end-points of the line XY in Figure 6.3. We shall soon see the use to which this construction can be put. Now relax the assumption that B_1 or B_2 is certain and return to the fact that our project yields either B_1 or B_2, each with a probability greater than zero and less than 1. Select some arbitrary values for these probabilities, say 0.4 for B_1 and 0.6 for B_2. Then the expected value of the outcome will be $0.4(B_1) + 0.6(B_2)$ and this will give us a point $\bar{B}$ in Figure 6.3. (To find such a point simply set the ratio $B_1\bar{B}/\bar{B}B_2$ equal to p_1/p_2.) Now, the utility that would correspond to B if it occurred with certainty would be $U(\bar{B})$, which is simply obtained by reading off the function $U(B)$. But the *expected utility* will be less because $\bar{B}$ is itself an expected value of the events B_1 and B_2. In fact, given equation (6.2), the value of EU is obtained by reference to the straight line XY, since equation (6.2) is in fact a linear function. In fact XY has the equation

$$EU = p_1 U(B_1) + p_2 U(B_2)$$

Now, another way of looking at $EU(\bar{B})$ is to observe that the same level of utility could be obtained from the *certain* occurrence of benefit B^*.

Armed with this analysis, we are now in a position to define some important concepts. We observe that $U(\bar{B})$ is greater than $EU(\bar{B})$, indicating that the utility from a benefit that occurs with certainty is greater than the utility that comes from an expected value of a benefit. Moreover, we can *measure* the cost of bearing the risk of the situation in which B_1 or B_2 occurs with degrees of probability. It is given by the distance $\bar{B} - B^*$, for B^* corresponds to the *certain* benefit which gives rise to the same utility as the 'gamble' (B_1 and B_2). We therefore define:

1. $\bar{B} - B^*$ = the 'cost of risk-bearing'
2. B^* = the 'certainty equivalent' of the gamble (B_1, B_2) which has the expected value $\bar{B}$.

The relevance for CBA is that we need to find the certainty-equivalent value of any probabilistic outcome. It is this certainty-equivalent value that we enter into the CBA. Incidentally, this is the same as inserting the expected value of the benefit and deducting the 'cost of risk-bearing'. To see this, simply deduct the cost of risk-bearing from the expected value of the benefit in the above analysis and we obtain

$$\bar{B} - (\bar{B} - B^*) = B^*$$

In our generalised cost–benefit formulae, then, we need to remember to insert, at all times, the certainty-equivalent values of costs and benefits. To bring the analysis back to our observations about means and variances, Figure 6.4 indicates essentially what is happening. It shows the expected value of benefits on the horizontal axis and the variance on the vertical axis. In order to accept higher and higher levels of variance, we find that society wants a very much greater value of $\bar{B}$. The 'indifference curve' between variance and expected value thus has the shape shown. But there will be a point on the benefits axis, B^*, which corresponds to a combination of zero variance and benefits B^*. Since the variance is zero, the magnitude B^* is certain. In other words, B^* is the certainty equivalent of all the combinations on curve i_1. There will be a family of such indifference curves. Thus i_0 shows one that is worse than i_1: for any level of B we see that a higher variance has to be tolerated compared with points on i_1. Hence i_0 is a lower indifference curve than i_1; and so on.

While we have a satisfactory analytical basis for dealing with risk in the CBA context, it will be observed that finding certainty-equivalent values of benefits and costs involves us in knowledge of society's utility function with respect to those benefits and costs. In practice, we have no procedure for observing these functions. Thus, while we know how we should take account of risk in an 'ideal' world, we are not really any more advanced in terms of practical measures for integrating risk into CBA.

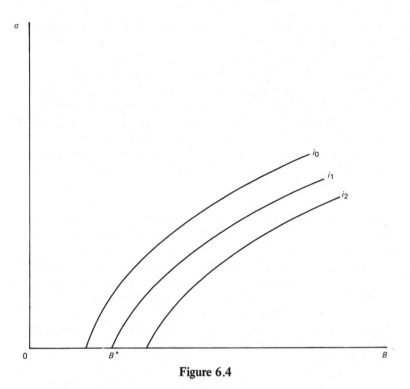

Figure 6.4

The Arrow–Lind theorem

We observed that if society could be regarded as risk-neutral, we could operate with the expected value of probabilistic benefit or cost estimates. If society is risk-averse, however, we require an estimate of the certainty-equivalent value of the cost or benefit. Since the latter procedure requires further estimation of a function relating money benefits (and costs) to social utility, however, it presents serious, if not insurmountable, difficulties for practical CBA. Clearly, it would be very convenient if CBA could assume risk-neutrality, for then we would have no need for an estimate of risk-bearing costs; we could use expected values of benefits and costs. One argument has been advanced which suggests exactly this, and it is known as the *Arrow—Lind theorem* (Arrow and Lind, 1970). What this theorem argues is that the larger the group of individuals across whom the risk is spread, the lower is the risk per head. This seems intuitively self-evident but a formal proof is complex. For what it involves is demonstrating that the risk *of the project* in question is itself reduced as the number of persons is increased. The Arrow—Lind theorem tells us that as the number of individuals approaches infinity, so the project risk approaches zero.

We offer no (formal or informal) proof here. A diagrammatic approach to the theorem is given in Pearce and Nash (1981). We satisfy ourselves with making a few observations on the result of the theorem. First, Arrow and Lind were concerned with the financial risk of projects in the public sector. For any nation the population across whom this risk is 'pooled' will be finite. Indeed, it should really be thought of as the taxpaying community, so that it might be 20 million in the United Kingdom and 80 million in the USA. These are large numbers, but obviously do not approach infinity! Thus the risk remains positive and not negligible.

Second, while financial risk can be pooled, many other risks that we need to deal with in CBA are not capable of being pooled even across the taxpaying population. This is because they are borne by groups of individuals who suffer the externality caused by the project in question. This may take the form of exposure to radiation, noise nuisance, air pollution, visual intrusion, congestion, and so on. The relevant group is thus the group of sufferers, and this will invariably be smaller than the nation's taxpayers. Hence the pooling argument appears to have even less force. One way of restoring some foundation to the argument is to point out, however, that compensation for such externalities could be borne by taxpayers. Thus the pooling of risk would again be restored.

The third qualification to the Arrow—Lind theorem was

pointed out by Fisher (1974). If the risk in question shows up in the form of a public 'bad' – i.e. an externality which is consumed equally by everyone, and where an increase in the 'consumption' of the externality by any one individual does nothing to reduce the consumption by others – then, however large the population, the risk is in no way reduced because it is constant across all individuals. Expanding the numbers of those exposed to the risk will not reduce the overall risk of the project, as the Arrow–Lind theorem would lead us to expect. Hence the theorem is applicable only to private goods and not to public goods or public bads (such as noise nuisance and the various examples given previously).

Uncertainty

While it is obvious that extensive thought has been given by economists to the analysis of risk, the preceding sections suggest that, in practical terms, the analytical procedures offer little by way of assistance. For this reason we can expect to find actual cost–benefit studies using simpler and cruder procedures. However, we need to look at the second major context in which benefits and costs are not known with certainty. This is the context of uncertainty in which the various possibilities are known but the probabilities of their occurrence are not known. Various rules have been advanced for dealing with these situations, and these rules emanate from *decision theory*. It is important to note that the rules do *not* allow us to 'collapse' variable estimates of costs and benefits into one indicator in the way that our certainty-equivalence analysis did. Because we have no probabilities to work with, we shall find that decision theory rules only really tell us what to do when we have set out the various net benefits under different assumptions about what will occur. That is, given various estimates of, say, benefits, we can estimate the final net benefit total that would accrue under each different assumption about individual benefit or cost estimates. As we shall see, many CBAs do this anyway, simply indicating what would happen to net social benefits if certain values are assumed for the uncertain items. Decision theory approaches, however, begin with this presentation. Typically, it is presented as a *pay-off matrix*. Table 6.1 shows such a matrix. Reading across, we have one source of the uncertainty, say the expected rate of economic growth. This will affect our benefit estimates in, say, a road project, by affecting our expectations about road traffic demand. The numbers 1 to 4 could then be percentage changes in real national income. Reading down Table 6.1 we have a second source of uncertainty which is some policy over which government has control. Notice that we do not have two 'uncontrollable' uncertainties. We have one which is not subject to control (the growth rate in our example) and one that is, which we refer to as 'policy'. We consider later what can be done when there are various sets of uncontrollable uncertainties.

Table 6.1

	Growth			
Policy	1	2	3	4
1	0	3	7	16
2	4	4	4	5
3	0	0	3	3
4	6	10	5	3

The main body of the matrix in Table 6.1 then shows the resulting net benefit figures. The net benefits do not simply increase with economic growth.

We may now consider the various rules that might be used.

These are:

1. *The 'maximax' criterion*

This is based on a very optimistic outlook. The aim is simply to go for the policy that maximises the net benefits (the 'pay-off'). In Table 6.1 we see that this is policy 1 because that has the potential for yielding net benefits of 16 units *provided* economic growth occurs at 4 per cent p.a. Note that it is also a very dangerous criterion because 1 per cent economic growth could occur and then net benefits will be zero. Since we cannot say what the probabilities are for economic growth we have no way of assessing the degree of danger in this approach, but clearly it is one that would only be undertaken by a confirmed gambler.

2. *The 'maximin' criterion*

In contrast to maximax, the maximin criterion is very cautious. What it does is to look at the *minimum* pay-offs under each strategy, and then choose the largest of these (i.e. it maximises the minimum pay-offs). In Table 6.1 we see that this would lead us to ring (mentally) the numbers 0 for policy 1, 4 for policy 2, 0 for policy 3, and 3 for policy 4. We then choose the maximum of these, which is 4 for policy 2, and hence we choose policy 2. In the case of the figures in Table 6.1, policy 2 could be argued to have some overall appeal because it does not have any zero pay-offs in it, and it is clearly superior to policy 3 under all circumstances. But in being cautious, policy 2 also missed the chance to go for the significantly larger benefits under policies 1 and 4.

3. *Index of pessimism*

Under this approach, we take the best and worst outcomes

for each policy. We then apply an 'index of pessimism' to the worst outcomes, which is in effect a subjective probability weighted by our feelings of cautions. In Table 6.1 we would select the following:

Policy 1 = 0,16
Policy 2 = 4,5
Policy 3 = 0,3
Policy 4 = 3,10

Suppose we set the index of pessimism at 0.9 and hence the index of 'optimism' at 0.1. Then, the calculations are as follows:

Policy 1 $(0.9 \times 0) + (0.1 \times 16) = 1.6$
Policy 2 $(0.9 \times 4) + (0.1 \times 5)\ \ = 4.1$
Policy 3 $(0.9 \times 0) + (0.1 \times 3)\ \ = 0.3$
Policy 4 $(0.9 \times 3) + (0.1 \times 10) = 3.7$

and the policy with the highest pay-off, i.e. policy 2, is chosen. The obvious problem with this approach is in setting the 'index of pessimism'. If it is set equal to unity, for example, it would be equivalent to selecting all the worst outcomes and would therefore be formally equivalent to the maximin criterion. If values different from unit are being used, one must question why this is any less complex than assigning subjective probabilities.

4. *Laplace criterion*

If we do not know the probabilities of any of the growth rates occurring, is this not the same as saying that each one is equally likely? This is what the so-called 'principle of insufficient reason' suggests, and what the criterion based on it, the Laplace criterion, would then suggest is that we simply assign a probability of 0.25 to each of the four growth rates. This would give weighted net benefits of

Policy 1 = 6.50
Policy 2 = 4.25
Policy 3 = 1.50
Policy 4 = 6.00

and policy 1 would be selected as having the highest pay-off. The criterion is misplaced, however, because if we do not know the probabilities we simply do not know them, and we cannot then deduce from a state of total ignorance something about the probabilities of events occurring!

5. *Minimax regret*

Again taking a cautious line we could look and see just what the cost of making a wrong choice will be. To do this we set up a 'regret' matrix, and the one corresponding to Table 6.1 is shown in Table 6.2

Table 6.2

Policy	Growth			
	1	2	3	4
1	6	7	0	0
2	2	6	3	11
3	6	10	4	13
4	0	0	2	13

To obtain the regret matrix, we read down the columns of Table 6.1. Suppose the growth rate turns out to be 1 per cent and we chose policy 1. The pay-off is 0. But had we chosen policy 4 with a growth rate of 1 per cent the pay-off would have been 6. Hence the 'regret' associated with the wrong choice of policy is 6. Similarly, had we chosen policy 2 the regret would have been $6 - 2 = 4$. That is, the regret is measured as the difference between the highest pay-off, given that a particular uncontrollable event occurs, and the pay-off that actually occurs. In this way we build up the regret matrix in Table 6.2. We then identify the maximum regrets and we see that these are, for the four policies in sequence, 7, 11, 13 and 13. We see the minimum of the maximum regrets ('making the best of a bad job') and thus choose policy 1.

Does this analysis help us? We have seen that different policies are chosen under different rules. Policy 1 was chosen under the maximax and the minimax regret rule. Policy 2 was chosen under the maximin and index of pessimism approach. We argued that the Laplace rule was inadmissible, but if it is used it would also choose policy 1. That different results are obtained from different rules is not surprising, however, since each embodies different attitudes to uncertainty. If society is risk-averse, we would not expect it to embrace the maximax criterion, leaving us with maximim and minimax regret. Coincidentally, in our example, minimax regret yields the same answer as maximax.

Other approaches to risk and uncertainty

The overriding impression we are left with is that there is no very satisfactory way of treating either risk or uncertainty in CBA. Typically, in practice, the adjustments made are of a much cruder nature than those we have suggested. But, equally, such adjustments are understandable given the limited usefulness of the techniques so far described. The main approach used for *uncertainty* is to make sure that ranges of estimates are given. In essence this reduces to presenting the results of a CBA in the form of the pay-off matrix similar to Table 6.1. However, instead of there being one controllable and one uncontrollable variable, we have two uncontrollable ones. For example, we might wish to test for the variation that will result if we have a range of estimates for the discount rate and a range of estimates for one item of benefit. Then a table like Table 6.1 can be constructed and the pay-offs can be shown. Obviously, uncertainty can extend to many items, in which case it becomes essential to look at what would happen with all combinations of assumptions. This approach is known as *sensitivity analysis* and is usually accompanied by the analyst's own 'best-guess' estimates.

A second approach is to apply a 'risk premium' to the discount rate. We observed that the discount rate has the effect of reducing the value of benefits and costs in terms of their present values, and the effect is greater the further into the future those costs and benefits occur. Since the uncertainty surrounding estimates of costs and benefits is often itself a function of time, it seems reasonable to make the discount rate serve two separate functions, the first of reflecting social time preference, and the second to reduce future money flows to reflect their uncertainty. In fact the exercise earlier in the chapter for calculating the cost of risk bearing can be adjusted to produce an estimate of the requisite risk premium. The procedure is outlined in Pearce and Nash (1981). However, even if we knew what addition to make to the social discount rate, there are some features of risk premia that make them unattractive. First, if the discount rate is, say, 5 per cent and we decide to add 2 per cent for risk purposes, we have effectively imposed a particular functional form of risk. We are saying that it has the form

$$p = e^{-0.02t}$$

where p is the premium and 2 per cent is the premium. The problem is that, set up in this way, we have imposed a time path on risk which may not be appropriate for the problem in hand. Second, if the risk in question relates to *costs*, we would wish to *add* to the cost element, not subtract from it. By adding a premium to the discount rate, however, we will be reducing costs simply because they are uncertain in size.

7

A Case Study: The Gordon-below-Franklin Dam

Chapters 1–6 have set out in outline form the main features of CBA. This chapter shows how some of those principles are applied in practice and the case study selected is the development of the Gordon River system in Tasmania, Australia, for the purposes of hydro-electric power. The project not only contains many fascinating issues in the application of CBA, it has also been the subject of a substantial protest from Australians and from the scientific and environmental community worldwide. The development would destroy an area of wilderness and some areas of outstanding scientific interest, including some containing evidence of early aboriginal settlement which, it is claimed, has significant archeological and anthropological interest. On the other hand, nearly all of Tasmania's electricity comes from hydro-power, and, at a time of high unemployment, the project offers the prospect of jobs. We thus have the classic 'trade-off' between the environment and direct economic gains.

The project

Figure 7.1 indicates in the broadest outline the nature of the scheme. The Franklin River flows into the Gordon River, which then flows into Macquarie Harbour. The section of the Gordon between the confluence of the Gordon and the Franklin is the 'Gordon-below-Franklin' River and the aim would be to build a dam and hydro-electric power station at the point marked 'PS' on the outline map. By so doing, the river waters would back up behind the dam and there would be flooding in the Gordon River back up to the existing Gordon Dam (shown as 'GD' in Figure 7.1). The Franklin and Olga Rivers would also be flooded for considerable lengths. Part two of the scheme would be to build a dam on the King River ('KD') to divert waters into the Franklin River system, and from there to the Gordon system. The additional effect would then be to flood other parts of the Franklin not affected by part one of the scheme. The map shows, very approximately, the areas affected by flooding (shown as the shaded area) and, of course, the flooded areas then serve as storage so that the power station can be controlled in terms of its throughput of water. Some of the areas shown already contain water storage from an earlier development, the Gordon River Power Development Stage One, which commenced full operation in 1978. The estimated output of the two new developments is 172 megawatts (one megawatt = 1,000 kilowatts) for the power station on its own, plus a further 168 megawatts if the King River diversion is included (Hydroelectric Commission of Tasmania, 1979). The scheme or schemes would be promoted by the Hydroelectric Commission of Tasmania, which has responsibility for generating and distributing Tasmania's electricity supply.

The benefits

The obvious benefit of the Gordon scheme is the output of electricity. As we saw, the proper way of approaching an

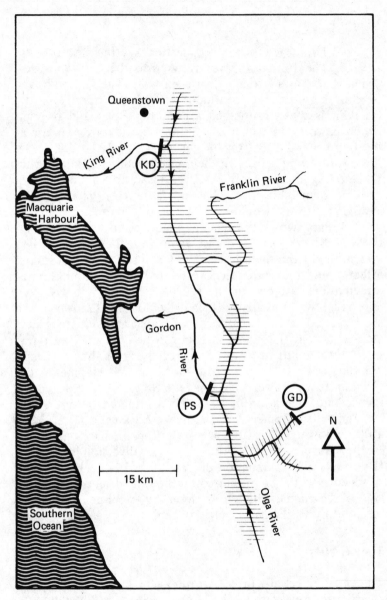

Figure 7.1

assessment of the benefits of any scheme is to estimate the consumer surplus involved. Now, in this case, such an estimate makes no particular sense unless we know what the *alternative* is to the hydro-electric schemes. The Hydroelectric Commission (HEC) considered alternative configurations of controlling the river systems, various 'alternative energy' approaches, such as tidal energy, and a conventional coal-fired power station of about 400 megawatt size, using imported coal from New South Wales. Last, the option of constructing a cable across the Bass Strait which separates Tasmania from Victoria was also considered, this cable carrying the necessary electricity from the mainland.

We consider the options in terms of a choice between the 'preferred' scheme, as described previously, and the construction of a coal-fired power station. HEC's argument was that the hydro scheme could continue to supply electricity at the same price as that which prevailed prior to the scheme, while adoption of the coal-fired power station would mean a higher charge for the electricity from that source. In short, coal-fired electricity was, it argued, more expensive than hydro-electricity. While some questions remain about the data sources used by HEC to come up with this general result, we shall accept it, along with other commentators on the proposal. However, HEC's analysis of the problem from here on must be replaced with that of independent economists simply because HEC's calculation of the extra cost borne by consumers has no foundation in economic analysis. We therefore follow Saddler, Bennett, Reynolds and Smith (1980) in their approach. This can be contrasted with the calculations of HEC.

Figure 7.2 shows the situation in respect of the demand for electricity. D_{1990} shows the demand curve in 1990 and this is seen to exhaust the capacity of the electricity system at price P_1, which we take to be the marginal cost of supplying electricity. If demand rises, then, we need to expand capacity and that is the point of the Gordon-below-Franklin scheme (or its alternative). Suppose the demand rises to D_{2000} by the year 2000 and that extra capacity is installed. If HEC is correct, it could supply the extra demand at the

93

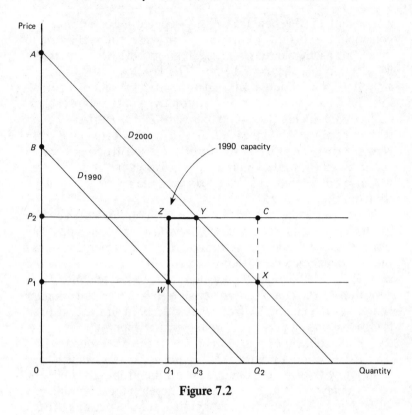

Figure 7.2

same price so long as it is allowed to invest in the hydro
scheme. Hence the quantity of electricity supplied would
change from Q_1 to Q_2. Now, if we measure consumer surplus
we see that, on the HEC analysis, it would increase from
BWP_1 to AXP_1. If the hydro scheme is implemented and
HEC's analysis is correct, surplus in 2000 would be AXP_1.
Now suppose that the hydro scheme is rejected and the coal-
fired plant is built. This has higher costs, given by P_2, assumed
equal to the marginal cost of producing electricity from coal.
Demand would now be Q_3 and the system would not be at
capacity if the coal-fired station has the same capacity as the

hydro project ($Q_1 Q_2$). At P_2 and Q_3 consumer surplus is now $A Y P_2$, which is *less* than that under the hydro scheme when, it will be recalled, it would be AXP_1 in 2000. By adopting the more expensive scheme, then, consumers would *apparently* 'lose' $P_2 Y X P_1$. But, as Saddler *et al.* note, the amount $P_2 Z W P_1$ is actually a *transfer* of surplus from consumers to the HEC. The HEC has effectively 'appropriated' some of the surplus through the higher charge, P_2, which now covers intra-marginal units (OQ_1) as well as marginal units of electricity. Since HEC has gained, there is no *net* loss to society with respect to the amount $P_2 Z W P_1$.

The consumer surplus loss from the more expensive option is thus $ZYXW$. This is the loss that Saddler *et al.* calculate. They note, however, that HEC's estimate of the cost to consumers is given by $ZCXW$, i.e. by the extra units of electricity that would be supplied if price were kept down to $P_1 (Q_1 Q_2)$ *multiplied by* the change in price ($P_1 P_2$). Clearly, this procedure exaggerates the consumer surplus loss by an amount YCX. The HEC failed to take into account the effect of the higher price of electricity on demand. Notice, of course, that if the change in price from P_1 to P_2 is very small, HEC's procedure would approximate the true loss.

The correct procedure is now to estimate the true loss of consumer surplus for each year from 1990 to the relevant 'time horizon', discount it back to a base year and sum the results to obtain the present value of the consumer surplus loss from the higher-cost electricity option. This, of course, is then formally equivalent to the consumer surplus gain from choosing the lower-cost hydro option. Obviously, the loss in, say, 1996, will not be the area shown in Figure 7.2 for the year 2000. To calculate the loss for each year therefore requires a projection of the demand for electricity so that we can estimate the demand curve for each year. This is what Saddler *et al.* do and the results are shown in Table 7.1.

Notice that two discount rates have been used, 5 per cent and 10 per cent. It is worth noting that assumptions about the price charged for electricity are not independent of the discount rate because the rate of return on capital is an integral part of the long-run marginal cost. Thus use of a higher discount rate not only reduces consumer surplus, because of the normal effects of a discount rate, but also because it raises the price P_2 in Figure 7.2. (It also should raise the price P_1.)

Table 7.1 *Consumer surplus gain to hydro scheme over coal-fired alternative (1980 Australian $ million)*

Type of demand	Saddler 5%	Saddler 10%	HEC 5%
General load	169.6	10.0	249.8
Industrial load	19.5	1.5	95.3
	189.1	11.5	345.5

Source: Saddler *et al.* (1980, p. 57).

Table 7.1 also shows the overall demand broken down into general (domestic, commercial) demand and industrial demand. This separation is not particularly important for our purposes, but exists because of the special importance of selected energy-intensive industries in Tasmania. The use of 10 per cent for a discount rate also reflects the fact that this is the rate recommended by the Australian Treasury Department. By any standards it seems high, and with Saddler *et al.* we prefer to focus on the results obtained using the 5 per cent analysis. Last, we observe that a comparison of the 5 per cent results by Saddler and those observed by HEC indicate the substantial nature of HEC's exaggeration of the surplus loss from adopting the coal-fired alternative. This arises because the cost differences between the hydro scheme and the coal-fired alternative are thought to be substantial.

The costs

The capital and operating costs of the two alternatives were estimated by both HEC and Saddler *et al.* For our purposes we need not investigate the procedures for obtaining these costs simply because the costs are already implicit in the prices used to calculate consumer surplus. That is, the benefits we are interested in have been measured net of the capital and operating costs. This means that we need only concentrate on the external costs in the form of loss of wilderness, etc. If these exceed the surplus gain from the hydro project, the hydro project is not worth while; and vice versa if they are less. The relevant figure to bear in mind, then, is the $A 189.1 million in Table 7.1. We need to know if wilderness costs are greater or less than this.

But there is an obvious problem in that we have no market in wilderness. We could interview people travelling to the area, though they are few and far between because of the nature of the terrain. Indeed, the 'virtue' of wilderness is that it is not visited by many people, otherwise it would cease to be wilderness. Yet we have noted that CBA, like all economics, is anthropocentric — it does not recognise values unless they are the value *of* human beings. This might suggest that the case against the hydro scheme in question is hopeless. There are no people to express any valuations!

The reference earlier to the outcry against the Gordon-below-Franklin scheme indicates a shortcoming of the view that people only value things by making some use of them. Scientists may well wish to visit particular sites of archeological and anthropological interest. Canoists, trekkers, etc., may well want to make use of the river systems as they are. Yet much of the outcry has never had its source among people who have either visited the area or who might even go there. It is sufficient for people to express concern about the area and their preference that it be left as it is for the analyst to identify the fact that there is a welfare loss to such people. The kind of valuation that emerges because individuals wish to retain an *option* to make use of a facility at some future date has been termed *option value*. It has been demonstrated that this option value will exceed the individual's expected consumer surplus from the facility in question. Indeed, option value is defined as the difference between an *option price* and the expected consumer surplus. This form of value was identified by Cicchetti and Freeman (1971), and a formal derivation of its relationship to consumer surplus is given in Pearce and Nash (1981). Other writers claim to have discovered other valuations as well. These include *existence value*, the value placed on the preservation of an asset regardless of wishing to exercise any option to make use of the asset, and *bequest value*, the value placed on an asset as something to be handed on to children and future generations. One or two studies claim to have measured the empirical magnitude of option, existence and bequest value, though it seems fair to say that substantial controversy surrounds the estimates obtained. (For an empirical study relating to water quality see Greenley *et al.*, 1981.)

The above concepts are sufficient to indicate that the absence of use of a wilderness area by no means implies that the area is not valued. None the less, it seems evident that exercises designed to 'reveal' these values will be complex. None has been undertaken for the Gordon dam example. Instead, Saddler *et al.* (1981) made use of a procedure developed by Krutilla and Fisher (1975). The next section offers a guide to the procedure developed by these authors (and others: the literature in question is now substantial).

Irreversibility

The essential point about the Gordon River development is that if the wilderness area is destroyed it cannot be reinstated. The cost of the destruction is thus *irreversible*. What can economics say about an irreversible loss? We could argue that no decision should ever be taken that entails an irreversible loss, but a moment's reflection will indicate just how stultify-ing this would be as a decision rule. Instead, we need to develop some mechanism for comparing costs and benefits. Equally, we have no obvious way of valuing irreplaceable assets such as species of wildlife, natural environments, and so on. What we *can* do is measure the benefits of the proposed development and at least ask the question whether the loss of wilderness, etc., is 'worth' the benefits obtained. But we need to formalise this simple approach, which, please note, makes no direct attempt to place a money value on the wilderness loss. It simply presents the choice to the decision-maker.

We now develop the basic ideas of the Krutilla and Fisher approach. In doing so, we make use of a synthesis produced by Porter (1982), which is not only an excellent survey of the work of Krutilla and his colleagues, but actually extends it in a number of interesting ways. We also use *perpetuities* for expositional purposes, just as we did when discussing discount rates in Chapter 4.

Consider a development project costing only $1. (We resort to the $ notation since this reflects the American literature which provides the basis for the approach that follows. It is also convenient because the $ is also the currency of Australia.) Let the development benefits from this project be $D per annum for ever. Then we can immediately write the present value of this project as

$$PV(D) = -1 + \int_0^\infty De^{-rt}dt \qquad (7.1)$$

where r is the discount rate.

Equation (7.1) reduces to

$$PV(D) = -1 + \frac{D}{r} \qquad (7.2)$$

Now, we need to compare the development benefits in (7.2) with the costs of the development. But bearing in mind the definition of cost as opportunity cost, it will be evident that the cost of the project is not simply the $1 expended on capital and operating costs of the development. It must also include the forgone benefits of the destruction of the environment as a natural asset. Let us call these benefits P per annum. Then the present value of these preservation benefits will be

$$PV(P) = \frac{P}{r} \tag{7.3}$$

and we shall have to write the net present value of the development project as

$$NPV(D) = -1 + \frac{D}{r} - \frac{P}{r} \tag{7.4}$$

For the development project to be admissible we require that $NPV(D)$ be greater than zero, i.e. on rearranging (7 4) we will have

$$\frac{D - P}{r} > 1 \text{; or } (D - P) > r \tag{7.5}$$

Now we can investigate the nature of the preservation benefits in a little more detail. First, we can observe that, over time, the *relative price* of P is likely to rise as the natural environment becomes less and less in quantity. Note that this is quite different from talking about general price rises. Those, as we saw earlier in the book, are not included in the CBA formula. But if we have reason to believe that any benefit or cost is likely to change its price significantly and relative to the general price level, then we should include that price rise in the analysis. This leads us to write the preservation benefit in year t as

$$P_t = P_0 e^{gt} \tag{7.6}$$

where P_0 is now the initial year's preservation benefit and g is the growth rate of the price of preservation benefits relative to the general price level. With Krutilla and Fisher (1975) we could go further and argue that our development scheme will

100

itself be subject to technological change which will render it less attractive through time. For example, hydro-electricity may become less attractive if nuclear power advances as a low-cost form of electricity. While this particular example, taken from the work of Krutilla and his colleagues, may seem suspect now, we use it only to demonstrate the general point that we may wish to discount the development benefits by a further factor, k, reflecting the rate of 'technological decay' of our project. Hence we would write:

$$D_t = D_0 e^{-kt} \tag{7.7}$$

If we now bring (7.6) and (7.7) together with the formula for $NPV(D)$, we shall have

$$NPV(D) = -1 + \int_0^\infty De^{-(r+k)t}dt - \int_0^\alpha Pe^{-(r-g)t}\, dt \tag{7.8}$$

which looks formidable, but reduces to

$$NPV(D) = -1 + \frac{D}{r+k} - \frac{P}{r-g} \tag{7.9}$$

(The observant reader may note that this will only be finite if we have r greater than g.)

Porter (1982) shows that equation (7.9) takes on positive values if, and only if,

$$\sqrt{D} > (\sqrt{P} + \sqrt{k+g}) \tag{7.10}$$

which is a result we take on trust for our purposes. If inequality (7.10) holds, then we find that the graph of present value against the discount rate, r, appears as in Figure 7.3. Here we see that net present value is positive only above a discount rate r_0 and below a discount rate r_1. In other words, the development project will succeed only if certain discount rates are adopted. High rates simply reduce the value of D in the normal way that discount rates affect benefits. Low rates tend to give the rate of growth g on the preservation benefits a chance to influence the choice against the development. Porter then shows that even small values of k and g will raise the required ratio of D to P if the development project is to proceed. For example, let P be (arbitrarily) 0.2 and let $k + g = 0.01$. Then inequality (7.10) tells us that, for the development to be worth while, D has to take a minimum value given by the inequality

$$\sqrt{D} = \sqrt{0.2} + \sqrt{0.01}$$

or

$$D = (0.536)^2 = 0.287$$

But this means that the ratio of D to P is $0.287/0.2 = 1.43$. That is, development benefits must be 43 per cent higher than preservation benefits for the development to be worth while. The result is therefore very sensitive to the important introduction of the 'new' features of the CBA, namely k and g.

Estimating required preservation benefits for the Gordon Dam

The preceding section provides the background to the calculations carried out by Saddler *et al.* (1980) in their assessment of what the preservation benefits would have to be for the Gordon River hydro project to be rejected. Saddler *et al.* engage in a more complicated analysis than that presented in the previous theoretical section. One reason for this is that wilderness value is unlikely to grow at the rate g for ever simply because we can expect actual users of the area to increase. Hence the area itself will have some 'limit' to its use set by congestion. Note that this is true only if we take account of *user values*. It is not true if what we believe we are projecting are option and existence values. Saddler *et al.* also build in the 'technological decay' factor in a manner somewhat different from that indicated by Krutilla and Fisher (1975) and Porter (1982). They argue that 'technological change will simply permit an increased availability of manu-

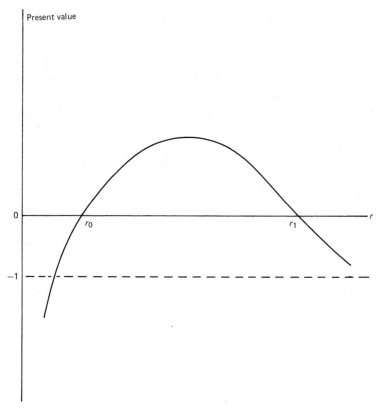

Figure 7.3

factured goods and services from a given source base, while the supply of the natural environment cannot be increased' (p. 81). This argument they use partly to justify the relative price increase, which we called *g*. While this is analogous to the 'decay' concept in the Krutilla–Fisher model, it is not quite the same, and indeed seems to suffer less from the criticism that can be made of the Krutilla–Fisher position, that the technological change affects the development project's benefits regardless of what happens to preservation benefits.

The net effect is similar, however, in that the compound growth factor for preservation benefits is augmented.

Various results are reported, depending on differing assumptions about the rate of growth of preservation benefits and differing discount rates. Taking the discount rate to be 5 per cent, the 'relative price effect' to be 4 per cent p.a. and the capacity of the region to absorb visitors to be reached in thirty years gives *the present value of $1 of initial-year preservation benefits* as $259.8. Now, to find out how large preservation benefits must be for the development project to be rejected, the procedure is as follows. First, we have an estimate of the consumer surplus gained by adopting the hydro project rather than the coal-fired power station, and that is $189 million. Second, we have the present value of $1 of preservation benefits and this is $259.8. Third, if we divide the former figure by the latter figure, we shall have obtained an estimate of what preservation benefits would have to be for them to equal the benefit of the hydro development. For, on division, we obtain

$$\frac{189,000,000}{259.8} = 727,483$$

What this means is that if the *initial year's* preservation benefits are, say, $750,000, then the present value of preservation benefits will be greater than the present value of the development benefits. Notice that we do not need to express the result in terms of benefits in each and every year. All that is being said is that if the benefits are $0.75 million in the first year, they will grow in the manner already described and will be greater than the consumer surplus lost from the choice of the more expensive coal-fired option.

This is what is meant when we said that preservation benefits did not have to be estimated directly. For all that we need is to present the results in this manner: do we believe that the wilderness, wildlife and areas of special interest lost because of the scheme have a value of $0.75 million *now*? If, for once, we step outside the cost–benefit analyst's shoes, it is difficult, surely, to believe that the answer is anything other than an emphatic 'yes'.

Epilogue

Since the Saddler *et al.* (1980) study, work has continued on the Gordon River proposal. No mention here has been made of employment, and this is a legitimate and worrying concern of Tasmanians and their government. The proper procedure, as we have seen, is to shadow price the labour that would be used in the project. But most likely to outweigh all other adjustments is the fact that the demand for electricity in Tasmania has been falling, as with most industrialised countries. In these circumstances the position of the demand curve D_{2000} in Figure 7.2 has changed and is to the left of what we have shown. But this means that the consumer surplus loss from choosing the higher-cost option is also reduced. From this it follows that the 'required' initial year's preservation benefits are also less.

In March 1983 Bob Hawke was elected Prime Minister of Australia. One of his first acts on taking office was to cancel the Gordon-below-Franklin hydro-electricity project.

References

K. Arrow and R. Lind (1970) 'Uncertainty and the evaluation of public investment decisions', *American Economic Review*, June.

A. J. Ayer (1936) *Language, Truth and Logic*, Gollancz, London.

B. Barry (1982) 'Intergenerational justice in energy policy', in D. MacLean and P. Brown (eds), *Energy and the Future*, Rowman & Littlechild, Totowa, New Jersey.

W. Baumol (1968) 'On the social rate of discount', *American Economic Review*, December.

M. Beesley *et al.* (1960) *The London–Birmingham Motorway – Traffic and Economics*, Road Research Laboratory Technical Paper No. 46, Department of Scientific and Industrial Research, London.

J. T. Bonnen (1966) 'The distribution of benefits from cotton price supports', in S. Chase (ed.), *Problems in Public Expenditure Analysis*, Brookings Institution, Washington.

C. Cicchetti and A. M. Freeman (1971) 'Option demand and consumer surplus: further comment', *Quarterly Journal of Economics*, August.

Commission on the Third London Airport (1971) *Report*, HMSO, London.

A. Dasgupta and D. W. Pearce (1972) *Cost–Benefit Analysis: Theory and Practice*, Macmillan, London.

J. Dupuit (1844) 'On the measurement of the utility of public works', *Annales des Ponts et Chaussées*, 2nd series, vol. 8, reprinted in English in D. Munby (ed.), *Transport*, Penguin, Harmondsworth, 1968.

O. Eckstein (1958) *Water Resource Development*, Harvard University Press, Cambridge, Mass.

M. Feldstein (1972) 'The inadequacy of weighted discount rates', in R. Layard (ed.), *Cost–Benefit Analysis*, Penguin, Harmondsworth.

References

A. C. Fisher (1974) 'Environmental externalities and the Arrow–Lind theorem', *American Economic Review*.

R. E. Goodin (1982) 'Discounting discounting', *Journal of Public Policy*, vol. 2.

J. V. de Graaf (1957) *Theoretical Welfare Economics*, Cambridge University Press, Cambridge.

D. Greenley *et al.* (1981) 'Option value: empirical evidence from a case study of recreation and water quality', *Quarterly Journal of Economics*, vol. 4, November.

J. R. Hicks (1939) 'Foundations of welfare economics', *Economic Journal*, December.

J. R. Hicks (1943) 'The four consumer's surpluses', *Review of Economic Studies*, vol. 11, Winter.

Hydroelectric Commission of Tasmania (1979) *Report on the Gordon River Power Development Stage Two*, Hobart, Tasmania.

R. Just, D. Hueth and A. Schmitz (1982) *Applied Welfare Economics and Public Policy*, Prentice-Hall, Englewood Cliffs, New Jersey.

N. Kaldor (1939) 'Welfare propositions of economic and interpersonal comparisons of utility', *Economic Journal*, September.

K. H. Katouzian (1980) *Ideology and Method in Economics*, Macmillan, London.

J. V. Krutilla (1981) 'Reflections of an applied welfare economist', *Journal of Environmental Economics and Management*, vol. 8.

J. V. Krutilla and O. Eckstein (1958) *Multiple Purpose River Development*, Johns Hopkins University Press, Baltimore.

J. V. Krutilla and A. C. Fisher (1975) *The Economics of Natural Environments*, Johns Hopkins University Press, Baltimore.

I. Little (1950) *A Critique of Welfare Economics*, Oxford University Press, Oxford (2nd edn 1957).

I. Little and J. Mirrlees (1969) *Manual of Industrial Project Analysis for Developing Countries*, OECD, Paris.

I. Little and J. Mirrlees (1974) *Project Appraisal and Planning for Developing Countries*, Heinemann, London.

A. Maass (ed.) (1962) *Design of Water Resource Systems*, Macmillan, New York.

A. Maass (1966) 'Benefit–cost analysis: its relevance to public investment decisions', *Quarterly Journal of Economics*, May.

References

M. McGuire and H. Garn (1969) 'The integration of equity and efficiency criteria in public project selection', *Economic Journal*, December.

R. McKean (1958) *Efficiency in Government through Systems Analysis*, Wiley, New York.

S. Marglin (1963) 'The opportunity costs of public investment', *Quarterly Journal of Economics*, May; and 'The social rate of discount and the optimal rate of saving', *Quarterly Journal of Economics*, February.

S. Marglin (1967) *Public Investment Criteria*, Allen & Unwin, London.

S. Marglin, A. Sen and P. Dasgupta (1972) *Guidelines for Project Evaluation*, UNIDO, Vienna.

E. J. Mishan (1974) 'Flexibility and consistency in project evaluation', *Economica*, February.

E. J. Mishan (1975) *Cost–Benefit Analysis*, 2nd edn, Allen & Unwin, London.

E. J. Mishan (1981) 'The nature of economic expertise reconsidered', in E. J. Mishan, *Economic Efficiency and Social Welfare*, Allen & Unwin, London.

E. J. Mishan (1982) 'The new controversy about the rationale of economic evaluation', *Journal of Economic Issues*, vol. 16, no. 1, March.

C. A. Nash, D. W. Pearce and J. Stanley (1975) 'An evaluation of cost benefit analysis criteria', *Scottish Journal of Political Economy*, June.

V. C. Nwaneri (1970) 'Equity in cost–benefit analysis: a case study of the Third London Airport', *Journal of Transport Economics and Policy*, September.

M. Olson and M. Bailey (1981) 'Positive time preference', *Journal of Political Economy*, February.

T. Page (1977) *Conservation and Economic Efficiency*, Johns Hopkins University Press, Baltimore.

A. Peacock (1973) 'Cost benefit analysis and the control of public expenditure', in J. N. Wolfe (ed.), *Cost Benefit and Cost Effectiveness*, Allen & Unwin, London.

D. W. Pearce (1983) 'Ethics, irreversibility, future generations and the social rate of discount', *International Journal of Environmental Studies*, April.

References

D. W. Pearce and C. A. Nash (1981) *The Social Appraisal of Projects*, Macmillan, London.

D. W. Pearce and J. Wise (1972) 'Equity in cost–benefit analysis: a comment', *Journal of Transport Economics and Policy*, September.

A. C. Pigou (1952) *The Economics of Welfare*, Macmillan, London.

P. Porter (1982) 'The new approach to wilderness preservation through benefit–cost analysis', *Journal of Environmental Economics and Management*, vol. 9.

F. Ramsey (1928) 'A mathematical theory of saving', *Economic Journal*, vol. 38.

J. Rawls (1972) *A Theory of Justice*, Oxford University Press, Oxford.

H. Saddler, J. Bennett, I. Reynolds and B. Smith (1980) *Public Choice in Tasmania*, Australian National University Press, Canberra.

E. F. Schumacher (1973) *Small is Beautiful*, Blond, London.

T. Scitovsky (1941) 'A note on welfare propositions in economics', *Review of Economic Studies*, November.

P. Self (1970) 'Nonsense on stilts: the futility of Roskill', *New Society*, 2 July.

P. Self (1975) *Econocrats and the Policy Process*, Macmillan, London.

A. K. Sen (1967) 'Isolation, assurance and the social rate of discount', *Quarterly Journal of Economics*, February.

L. Squire and H. van der Tak (1975) *Economic Analysis of Projects*, Johns Hopkins University Press, Baltimore.

UK Government (1967) *Nationalised Industries: A Review of Economic and Financial Objectives*, Cmnd 3437, HMSO, London.

B. Weisbrod (1966) 'Income redistribution effects and benefit–cost analysis', in S. Chase (ed.), *Problems in Public Expenditure Analysis*, Brookings Institution, Washington.

R. D. Willig (1976) 'Consumer's surplus without apology', *American Economic Review*, vol. 66, no. 4, September.

Index